D0941474

# VICTORY OVER SUFFERING

Books by A. Graham Ikin
published in the United States of America

LIFE, FAITH AND PRAYER. *Oxford University Press, New York. 1954.*

NEW CONCEPTS OF HEALING: MEDICAL, PSYCHOLOGICAL AND RELIGIOUS. *Association Press, New York. 1956.*

# VICTORY OVER SUFFERING

## *Glimpses into a Mystery*

★

by

A. GRAHAM IKIN

★

FOREWORD BY J. B. PHILLIPS

INTRODUCTION BY EDWARD ELY

Published by Channel Press, Inc.,
Great Neck, New York

Library of Congress Catalog Card Number: 61-7572

LITHO IN U. S. A.

# FOREWORD

## By J. B. Phillips

The problems aroused by human suffering are, to my mind, the biggest difficulties that the intellectually honest Christian ever has to face. Many healthy extraverted people apparently live in happy ignorance of these problems, or possibly instinctively avoid them in the same way that certain animals will avoid a sick or wounded companion. But there are millions who have the problem of suffering thrust upon them, either personally or in their family circle. And there are, thank God, many people who feel the tragedy of the human predicament, and many who devote themselves to the alleviation of human suffering, although they are frequently without any consciousness that they are co-operating with the Purpose of God.

Nevertheless, many ordinary people find the spectacle of innocent suffering a denial of the existence of a loving God, and spend their days in an unhappy agnosticism. Many others go on resignedly, frequently with most moving courage, but unable to see any point or purpose in human suffering.

Miss Ikin faces the problem fairly and squarely, and I would venture to say that a book such as this could never have been written unless the writer herself had had first-hand experience of suffering. In one sense, there is nothing new in this book, but it is written with such quiet courage and such downright honesty and above all with such hopefulness that it cannot help suggesting to those who think and feel better ways of facing the issue than dogged resignation or unhappy agnosticism.

Quite rightly the central theme of the book is that the God whom Christians worship is Himself a Suffering God. There is not a morbid word throughout the book, but a quiet insistence that we cannot begin to understand, or indeed to endure, suffering until we have deepened our insight into the Character of God Himself.

There are no facile answers here, because there are no facile answers, and Miss Ikin is too honest to offer mere sops for the sorrowful. But there is plenty to stimulate courage and hope, and plenty to deepen the understanding of both thinker and sufferer alike. This is no book for the superficial, but for those who are prepared to use their minds and hearts it may well give some fresh glimpse of the vast Divine Pattern which will prove infinitely reassuring. To read what Miss Ikin has to say on this oldest of human problems will certainly reward the diligent seeker after Truth.

# INTRODUCTION

THIS IS NOT AN EASY BOOK: NOR IN ANY SUPERFICIAL WAY WILL it make us feel comfortable: but I believe it will bring comfort and help to many.

At the beginning of Chapter IV Miss Ikin emphasises that she is writing with a view to the needs of ordinary men and women engaged in earning a living and running a home and most of what she writes deals directly and simply with our ordinary needs. A great deal of the suffering in the world, as she says, is a consequence of our "sins, negligences and ignorances", not a punishment but a consequence.

Miss Ikin does not claim to solve the mystery of suffering completely: that may not be possible in this life: but she points a way to facing it creatively, in the Light and Power of Christ's Resurrection. This is the pledge of the Power of Love to triumph over the worst consequences of its own betrayal, and therefore over the worst suffering that can befall us.

Miss Ikin writes from her own experience of winning through suffering to some creative insights which have enriched not only her own life but that of others. She has not only suffered in her own personal life: but in her dealings with others she has learnt much about the suffering of others; and there has, as always, been pain in the sharing.

Some may find one or other chapter difficult to understand, but none of us for that reason should think that the book is "beyond us". It speaks to the heart and not only the head: and all may find a word that "speaks to their condition" somewhere within the whole. All the problems involved are squarely faced, not evaded, and the heart of the problem is reached in "Why Do the Innocent Suffer?"

Those of us who, as doctors, teachers or pastors, are called on to help others must be conscious again and again of our inadequacy to the task. I believe others, like myself, will find food here for thought and action. There is much sound moral theology in the book: though expressed simply for the many who might be put off by technical terms. But as Miss Ikin says, "There is no short cut". Life has to be lived out, not just thought out; though sound thinking is essential to right living. The book arises out of life and indicates a way of life that challenges the materialism and pessimism prevalent to-day.

We deal with a great mystery: suffering has always been, as Miss Ikin says, "the greatest challenge to belief in a good God". She tries to show that though it calls for courage in the living, there are grounds for faith and hope that our sufferings and struggles are not in vain, and that we may see them "as we saw it on Calvary, as the greatest proof that Love is the supreme value, the supreme quality of the very Being of God, and that through it He evokes in us a dim image of His own Divine Compassion, and when we awake in His likeness, we shall be satisfied with it".

EDWARD ELY

# AUTHOR'S PREFACE

ANYONE WHO ESSAYS TO THROW SOME LIGHT ON THE MYSTERY of suffering in a world that is also shot through and through with beauty, and in which our human minds are so constituted that to them "truth matters", needs to give some hints of his credentials and experience.

A world disillusioned by two world wars after expecting unbroken progress, and gripped by the fear of a third, will no longer accept pious platitudes or the "inscrutable will of God" as explanations.

Welfare states and hydrogen bombs do not mix well. Yet at the moment we are involved in the mixture which expresses the culmination of the development of two different ways of life, each claiming a measure of our allegiance.

The split between East and West is not just a geographical, nor even a purely historical one. It is a cleavage within mankind which has over-emphasised some truths on each side and thus partly neutralised their influence by ignoring the greater whole of which they form a part.

This is not necessarily evil in itself. Our human minds grow steadily through the ages and to grasp some new truth, some new facet of Reality, it must be temporarily spot-lit, which throws the matrix out of which it emerged back into the shadows.

The following quotation shows how longstanding this difficulty is and the need for some fresh vision to "see life steadily and see it whole".

*The Disagreement as to the Description*
*and Shape of the Elephant*[1]

[1] From the book of Sufi wisdom *The Mathnawi* of Jalalu'ddin Rumi. Quoted by Kenneth Walker in *The Diagnosis of Man*, p. 13.

The elephant was in a dark house: some Hindus had brought it for exhibition.

In order to see it, many people were going, every one, into that darkness.

As seeing it with the eye was impossible, each was feeling it in the dark with the palm of his hand.

The hand of one fell on its trunk: he said, "This creature is like a water-pipe."

The hand of another touched its ear: to him it appeared like a fan.

Since another handled its leg, he said, "I found the elephant shape to be like a pillar."

Another laid his hand on the back: he said, "Truly this elephant was like a throne."

Similarly, when anyone heard a description of the elephant, he understood it only in respect of the part that he had touched.

On account of the diverse place of view their statements differed: one man entitled it "dal", another, "alif".

If there had been a candle in each one's hand, the differences would have gone out of their words.

The eye of sense-perception is only like the palm of the hand: the palm hath not power to reach the whole of the elephant.

The eye of the Sea is one thing, and the foam another: leave the foam and look with the eye of the Sea.

Day and night there is movement of foam-flecks from the Sea: thou beholdest the foam, but not the Sea. Marvellous!

All our cross-sections of Reality are like this. They are real points of contact with the Whole that unites them. It is fruitless to waste time standing out for any particular finite viewpoint as exclusive or total, or quarrelling with those who from another viewpoint have seen another aspect. We need to pool our partial insights, not ignoring others, nor deprecating or apologising for our own, but accepting each as valid within its own sphere and making its own contribution to the integrated complexity of the whole.

Suffering, which is so inescapable, may thus find its significance within the greater whole that transcends it and so throw light on the nature of the Whole which includes it creatively, and brings greater values into being through its challenge to life, to faith, to security and to love.

My credentials for thus attempting to throw some light into, or onto, a mystery that concerns us all are two-fold. Much of my work has been connected with that of doctors, clergy and ministers, and with the practical problems of co-operation between them to relieve distress more effectively.

Some of the deepest insights into this, however, have come through suffering in my own life. Looking back, though I could not have chosen so hard a road from the start, I can see that some of the heights of the "ups" in life have been proportional to gains made during the "downs" which at the time seemed to have checked both life and usefulness. Such insights, however, did not come automatically, but through a real involvement in and grappling with the mystery of suffering itself.

The term "mystery" may at first sight seem strange in this connection. Yet no other term holds together the bewildering paradox that the very suffering and distress which challenge belief in the goodness of God can lead to a deeper awareness of a purpose that transcends the suffering and transmutes it into a participation in a life that is creative of fellowship on a wider scale than family or nation.

From every side the need is to recognise the range of God's activities not only within the sphere of religion as narrowly conceived, but within the whole creation. Emphasis on the Atonement, on the sufferings of Christ, has sometimes dimmed the wonder of the reality of His Incarnation, of the quality of the life of the Spirit lived in and through the Flesh, which blessed the ordinary conditions of daily life, and hallowed them. Christ, for the joy that was set before Him, endured the Cross. He so often spoke of joy, that His joy might be in us, a joy no man taketh away from us.

This book is written in the hope of helping many who are in distress, of body or mind, to win through to a realisation that there is a "Light that shines in the darkness". The darkness cannot finally eclipse it because it is the Light of the Eternal God breaking through into our world of space and time and humanity to redeem it and bring it to the fullness of perfection foreseen in the Mind of God.

The style in the first four chapters differs in some respects from that in the rest of the book. The necessity for providing a sound basis in the earlier chapters for what is built upon them needed a different approach. If readers are aware of this they may get equal benefit from *both*. Too many religious books plunge into the subject on the assumption that their premises as to the reality and nature of God are accepted by the reader. To-day, however, with so many more people questioning this in the light of concentration camps and hydrogen bombs within Christendom, as well as the differences amongst Christians themselves, it is necessary to start from a more elementary level and build from that, if these people are to look at and gain from the practical approach in the later chapters. It is hoped in this way to provide a basis for the genuinely perplexed as well as some illumination for those who may have gone farther along the way of Christian living. Theory and practice intertwine, in life as well as in thought.

* * *

"Why Do the Innocent Suffer?" shows how the very consequences of the "sins, negligences and ignorances" of mankind, which fall on the guilty and the innocent alike, can lead to an awakening of spiritual qualities such as patience, compassion and love that could not develop if all suffering was merited punishment which it would be wrong to alleviate.

"Hidden Wounds" shows how much mental and emotional suffering goes on behind the scenes. It also stresses the need for emotional honesty with ourselves, if these hidden wounds are not to poison our lives. Rightly faced they deepen our spiritual roots, and by so doing open up to us wider reaches of reality than to those living more superficially.

"Break Out, Break Down or Break Through" shows the possibility of differing reactions to "crises", which always combine danger and opportunity. Our fundamental attitude largely decides whether we run away from or face up to danger and so lose or profit by the opportunity.

After getting a clue through facing up to the tragic element in life, "Life's Common Ways" brings the problems down into the everyday living, with which most of the time we are concerned.

The next chapter deals with guilt and forgiveness. This is a problem with which all of us are faced. It shows how guilty emotions, bitterness and resentment blind us to reality and distort our vision, and so block the way to the free flow of the spirit which is released by a forgivingness based on having found our own forgiveness for our part in the evils of the world.

In order to follow Christ's way of triumphing over and through suffering, however, we need some "Guidance in Living". This chapter shows many of the routine ways through which God actually guides, which we may not always recognise as His at all.

This leads on in "Further Glimpses of How God Guides" to a conscious seeking for His guidance in prayer and meditation. This in turn leads on to a deeper level of interior awareness of a Divine quickening or response to our need in a chapter on "How to Know the Will of God". Here a personal series of meditations is used to illustrate the illumination that came as a response to a whole-hearted attempt to discover how to discriminate between the promptings of our own subconscious desires and the true impact of the Mind of God upon us.

"The Spiritual Factor in Healing" shows the central importance for life and health of the spiritual matrix of our life on earth. Healing is a "making whole" so that the physical, mental and spiritual components of our human make-up can function harmoniously.

This in turn shows the need for a "Pattern in the Cosmos" which is not imposed *by* man, but is *discovered* by him in the Cosmos or Universe in which he lives as a small but real part.

"Over-ruling Providence and Religious Experience" illustrates the way in which this fundamental pattern can be recognised and realised in our daily lives, to their great enrichment. A new dimension of life is found to be as genuinely rooted in Reality as the more superficial one within which, apart from religion, we seem to be confined.

"The Chain-mail of the Spirit" illustrates some ways in which this interaction or interpenetration of the horizontal or temporal with the vertical or eternal aspects of reality brings a fullness of life here and now.

This is followed up in "The Good that has No Opposite" by showing that temporary evils, however great, are not permanent elements in the Cosmos. They are accompaniments of a creative Process that is fundamentally Good. As this progressively overcomes the uncontrolled "release phenomena" by a redemptive activity that restores them to their true potentialities, the suffering involved is transmuted into the joy of overcoming and unlimited vistas for growth and development are glimpsed.

"In His Name" illustrates the significance of the Name as expressing the inner reality of Being. Thus Christ could promise that all prayers in His name would be answered, because there was the power to perform all that could reach that central focus of God on earth. In Him the Divine image in man was one with its Divine source, undistorted by sins, negligences or ignorances.

The last chapter on "The Invisible Christ" reveals other aspects of this pattern that could not be discovered by man on the natural level. This gives the hope of ever closer approximation to it as we follow in His footsteps, with increasing power to overcome and eliminate the distortions of the pattern which cause so much suffering.

L'Envoie, in the words of Albert Schweitzer, shows the reality of the "Fellowship of His Sufferings" which expressed the ineffable mystery of a life that transcends them and in its deepest essence is wholly good.

*Eskdale, Cumberland*
1957

A. GRAHAM IKIN

## CONTENTS

# ACKNOWLEDGMENTS

The author is grateful to the following persons and publishers who have granted permission for reprinting copyright material:

W. H. Allen & Co. for quotations from *Faith is Power* by Daniel A. Poling.

H. T. Hamblin, Science of Thought Press, for a quotation from *In the Desert a Highway* by Richard Whitwell.

Arthur James Ltd. for quotations from *Everyman's Mission* by Dr. Rebecca Beard, *I will Lift Up Mine Eyes* by Professor Glenn Clark, *The Healing Light* by Agnes Sanford, and *Christ Still Healing* by Elsie H. Salmon.

Macmillan & Co. and Mrs. Temple for quotations from *Nature, Man and God* by the late Dr. William Temple.

Methuen & Co. and Miss Oxenham for a quotation from *Bees in Amber* by the late John Oxenham.

Max Parrish Ltd. for quotations from *A Doctor's Faith Holds Fast* and *A Doctor's Faith is Challenged* by Dr. Christopher Woodard.

Vincent Stuart Publishing Co. for a quotation from *Living Time* by Maurice Nicoll.

James Clarke & Co. for quotations from *Healing Through the Power of Christ* by the Rev. Dr. Jim Wilson.

The Editors of *The Guild of Health Monthly*, the *Methodist Magazine* and the *Science of Thought Review* for permission to include in this book some of my work previously published by them.

I

# WHY DO THE INNOCENT SUFFER?

MUCH OF THE SUFFERING IN THE WORLD IS DUE TO IGNORANCE. Centuries ago, about the time that Deutero-Isaiah was spiritualising the Jewish religion, Buddha was doing the same in India. Isaiah and the other Jewish prophets stressed moral evil as the cause of suffering, while Buddha stressed ignorance of the true nature of life as its cause. Isaiah worked out the conception of the Suffering Servant as bearing the burdens of the sin of others, through which vicarious suffering—the voluntary suffering of the innocent—the cause of suffering in sin was annulled. Buddha sought enlightenment, a release from the ignorance at the root of both sin and suffering, and so sought to eliminate both sin and suffering through participating in the true nature of Reality.

Christ combined the insights of both these great spiritual leaders. He explicitly ruled out sin as the *only* cause of disease. "And as he passed by, he saw a man blind from his birth. And his disciples asked him, saying, Rabbi, who did sin, this man, or his parents, that he should be born blind? Jesus answered, Neither did this man sin, nor his parents: but that the works of God should be made manifest in him."[1] He then proceeded to cure his blindness.

Moreover, in connection with accident, He said: "Or those eighteen, upon whom the tower in Siloam fell, and killed them, think ye that they were offenders above all the men that dwell in Jerusalem? I tell you, Nay: but except ye repent, ye shall all likewise perish."[2]

[1] John 9, vv. 1–3. [2] Luke 13, vv. 4–5.

His call to repentance to all, irrespective of whether they were recognised as sinners or keeping the law rigorously externally yet were uncharitable at heart, was a call to *metanoia*, as the Greek stresses. This is a call to a change of mind, a new way of looking at things. The call to "watch" in "watch and pray" is better translated as "to be awake", as if the everyday life was like being asleep. This is a call to seek "enlightenment", to become aware. Dr. Rebecca Beard put this beautifully in her seven steps of meditation—the seven A's: Awake, Aware, Acutely awake and aware, Alert, Alive, Attuned, At-one.[1]

It is a call to awareness of a spiritual dimension of being going beyond the merely natural. This is a spiritual life that does not destroy but fulfils the natural; yet which the natural life of man cannot give rise to of itself. It is the "gift of God". Christ said, "And ye shall know the truth and the truth shall make you free".[2] Socrates and Buddha had realised the ultimate value of truth centuries before. But Christ embodied or incarnated the Truth, uniting the natural and the spiritual, the human and the Divine in a way that also enabled Him to say "I am the Way, and the Truth, and the Life".[3]

Christ obviously distinguished different kinds of suffering. We read that He was "moved with compassion" and He spent much of His time actually healing sick people. We never hear Him say God sent sickness. When He had healed a woman who had been unable to straighten her back and lift herself up, and been attacked by the ruler of the synagogue for doing so, He said, "Ought not this woman, being a daughter of Abraham, whom Satan had bound, lo, these eighteen years, to have been loosed from this bond in the day of the sabbath?"[4]

Yet He did call His disciples to take up their cross to follow Him, and a cross in those days meant the literal reality of an agonising and cruel death. It was not the sign of victory it has

[1] *Everyman's Search*, pp. 112–14. Publishers: Arthur James.
[2] John 8, v. 32.
[3] John 14, v. 6.
[4] Luke 13, v. 16.

become for us since Christ hung on it Himself and yet could not be bound by it.

There was a challenge to overcome the cause of suffering. It is here we find the supreme paradox that Christ's voluntary acceptance of the consequences of the worst the evil in the world could inflict actually transformed them from signs of destruction and hate into a manifestation of the love that triumphed in and through the death of the body and set free a Spirit that is slowly but surely leavening the world. This Spirit of Christ is not a vague ideal; it is not a phantasy or mirage; it is the Spirit that won its freedom from the bondage of sin and death by surviving death in a form and personality that was recognisably one with the life on earth that preceded it. *God entered into humanity completely enough to raise humanity to another plane of life, to take manhood into God.* The new humanity is not discontinuous with the old. It is not something merely superposed on it from above. It transforms the raw material of the old way of life, the old level of life. It transfigures it so that it can fulfil the purpose of God for mankind. We can then respond effectively to His will and find in so doing the fulfilment of the potentialities within mankind that can come to full fruition only within the fellowship of the Holy Spirit.

This fellowship is composed of those whose centre of gravity, so to speak, is in the common world of Spirit and not in the self-centred world of natural man. Most of us are in a state of transition. Sometimes we are dragged back by elements in us that are as yet imperfectly spiritualised. Sometimes we are lifted onto a level of experience which we intuitively recognise as a more adequate fulfilment of our nature than that on which we had been living. This, however, we usually find we can only reach intermittently at first. But every such glimpse spurs us on to bring all that is in us under the control and direction of the Christ Spirit who has given us the pledge and guarantee of ultimate fulfilment if we follow Him along the trail He blazed for us.

Sick people often say that only those who have themselves suffered seem able to understand and help, as only they know what it feels like. It is true that the normally healthy individual whose body will carry him round to do what he wants to do without his having to be aware of it, really cannot imagine what it is like to have a body that is not responsive. He thinks of reaching for his pipe and automatically his hand goes out to reach it. Someone with a crippled or partly paralysed arm may want his pipe, but he has to think not only of reaching it, but of how to make the necessary movements with effort, pain and difficulty.

So, too, someone who has been brought up in a happy home and grown into a self-confident reliable person may find it difficult to understand someone whose childhood had been so filled with fear that self-confidence could never be achieved. Later in life, failure after failure dins in the lesson to such a one that life is a terrible thing. To the first, life is a privilege, a joy: to the second it may be a nightmare. Yet to both of these Christ can speak as one who has "come through". The Christ who fell under the load of a cross, as His body could no longer respond to the demands made on it, understands the one whose illness makes little things, that are so much child's play to the healthy, an effort that he can only maintain for short periods. Christ, Who, on the cross, cried out, "My God, My God, why hast Thou forsaken me?", can share the bewildered feeling that life is a nightmare.

God, for anyone, stands for the highest we can know or can imagine: to feel deserted by God is to feel the bottom has dropped out of the familiar world and nothing worth while seems to be left. This experience comes in some form to many under the shock of sudden bereavement or betrayal. Yet Christ has been that way too before us, and can, as no other, stand by us in our agony with the *knowledge*, not just faith or hope, that "underneath are the Everlasting arms", and that *nothing* God has created can destroy the foundations He has laid. Christ could emerge through the darkness, trusting again the God by whom He had felt deserted, saying, "Father, into Thy Hands I commend my Spirit". His Resurrection proved that trust had not been in vain.

Something had been achieved in that brief spell that bound God and man together in a fellowship that can never be broken. *God won't let go!* He is with us in our worst, as well as our best. Our trust is not in ourselves but in Him who made us.

For a long time man projected his idea of what God or the gods were like, making God in his own image. But idol after idol, false picture after false picture, was broken down by the Ultimate Reality responsible for making both man and the world within which he lives, until *in Christ we see the image of God in man.* After that we can begin to let God re-make us into His image, as He has been preparing to do as soon as we could grasp the idea of sonship and not automatic or mechanical obedience to a Power so infinitely greater than our own.

Sins, negligences and ignorances are *all* causes of suffering, not only to ourselves but to others. But sin can be repented of, negligence can be replaced by responsibility, and ignorance can lead to a search for truth. The causes of suffering are not irredeemable: they are not inevitable and they are not elements in the eternal destiny of mankind. They are incidental to the temporal processes of growth. With the reaching of full maturity they are transcended. Christ's life, taking into and onto Himself all the consequences of the sins, negligences, and ignorances of mankind in Gethsemane and on Calvary, blazed the trail to the new life by His Resurrection.

This is the life of the new age that can no longer be bound by the sin of the past and which replaces negligence by responsibility. Christ faced and accepted a painful death which revealed the truth and reality of a Spirit that could triumph in and through the worst suffering anything in the transitional, temporal contingent world could inflict. In *His* strength, by the power of His Spirit, we too can wrest victory from our defeats.

We are all involved in the mingled good and evil in and around us. We all at times find the consequences of evil in some form are more than we can bear without suffering. This may involve the breakdown of our defences in illness of body through lowered resistance to infections. It may involve illness of mind, which turns us in on ourselves until we see the whole world through distorting spectacles. It may involve illness of spirit, which blinds us to the resources of spirit from another dimension. This cuts us off for the time being from the help of reinforcements which were actually available.

Some suffering in our own lives we can see is the consequence of our own actions; though even then these may seem to be out of all proportion to our actual responsibility. But other suffering seems to fall on us independently of anything we have done and to be such that we could not in any way have averted. The suffering of little children seems to be an indictment of God to which we must find some answer.

Yet this, too, is part of the mystery of suffering which binds us into a fellowship which is independent of age, race, sex or the period in which we live and so enables us to transcend our petty selves. This is the raw material out of which, both in suffering endured and in suffering incurred in the attempt to relieve that of others, the Kingdom of Heaven can be brought on earth. We need to realise this really is a kingdom, not a series of totally independent individuals. We hear of flood or famine in some distant part of the world, and flood or famine relief funds are set up at once to help the victims. In the presence of calamity, a pit disaster, an earthquake or a flood, the true impulse of humanity breaks through the self-seeking and self-concern of competitive life and shows it is not the last word, even in us. Something of the Spirit of our Father breaks through. The many devoted workers amongst the heartbreaks of refugees, of dispossessed and displaced persons, of nurses and doctors who see so much agony and anguish in the course of their work in trying to alleviate it, witness to this. They show there is a creative power in suffering. This is a true mystery and we should be the poorer *as a race* if the suffering of the innocent did not stir us to take steps to ameliorate or avert it where possible.

If only the guilty suffered we might think God was a God of Justice, but the deeper attributes of Mercy and Compassion would be lacking. It is actually because God *is* Love that the innocent as well as the guilty suffer. We suffer for the sins, negligences and ignorances of others, as they must do for ours. In the second commandment we have a glimpse of this; the sins of the fathers are visited on the children to the third and fourth generation, that God's mercy may be shown to thousands of those who love Him. There is no way of ensuring the entail of good without an entail of evil wherever this becomes *actual* in terms of either sin, negligence or ignorance. The passing on to others of the fruits of man's labours, of the rise in the standard of living not only on the material but on the spiritual level, shows the reality of the good. But we could learn nothing, take no responsibility without the abiding consequences of our actions, both for good and for evil. But the mercy of God has constructed the framework within which mankind is set so that the very consequences of evil lead us to try to find how to avert them. It also ensures that the consequences of evil are less durable than those of good. A degenerate stock, suffering for the sins of its fathers, may end with the idiot who is sterile, and that stock no longer infects the race. The heirs of good stock spread their influence more widely as each finds itself linked with the "thousands who have not bowed the knee to Baal".

We so often ask when things go wrong with us "Why should this happen to me?" and forget all the good things that have come our way through the love and labour of others that we had neither earned nor deserved, but just taken for granted.

We benefit in this way through all the work of others who build the houses in which we live, grow the food we eat, make the material for the clothes we wear, and write the books we read. But this involves having to share in consequences of the lack when some hitch occurs either in distribution or production. We often only realise how much of our own success had depended on the lives and work of others when some element in this is withdrawn. We then realise we cannot be self-sufficient and have no room for self-satisfaction.

Moreover, if only the guilty suffered, self-righteousness would be an inevitable accompaniment on the part of the innocent. This would be more harmful to the spiritual life than bearing the consequences of the sins of others which opens the door to forgiveness and the recognition of something of value in each human being that goes deeper than *any* sin. When innocent and guilty suffer, we realise there may be much in the history of those who can be seen to be the aggressors, the murderers, the adulterers, the thieves or embezzlers that may have been the result of the sins of others, and temper justice with mercy.

This will be considered more fully in the chapter "Break Out, Break Down or Break Through?" It is enough if in this chapter we have seen a golden thread running through the blackness of the suffering of the innocent. This is the consequence of our organic solidarity with the animal and vegetable worlds on which our bodies depend for food: as well as on our social solidarity with the whole of mankind as we share a common history and a common heredity. We can only share in the results of the insights and creative activities of others if we also share in the consequences of our respective sins, negligences and ignorances. Finally, the eternal value of the self-sacrifice of Christ in redeeming or bringing back to its true nature those in whom it has been distorted, shows the central significance of the suffering of the innocent for God Himself, as part of the very existence of love.

The suffering of the innocent has always been the greatest challenge to belief in a good God. Here we see it at last, as we saw it on Calvary, as the greatest proof that love is the supreme value, the supreme quality of the very Being of God and that through it He evokes in us a dim image of His own Divine compassion, and when we awake in His likeness we shall be satisfied with it.

## II

# HIDDEN WOUNDS

HOW LITTLE EVEN OUR BEST FRIENDS MAY REALISE OF WHAT IS going on behind the scenes of our lives while we are trying to put a brave face on some tragic happening that, for the time being, has knocked the bottom out of our world. There are hidden wounds in many lives. The theme of this chapter was suggested to me by a letter from a young friend who had lost her father unexpectedly by accident, in which she said she felt she could not put on a "false front" to me and had to write as she was really feeling, which was very different from the appearances she was trying to keep up.

Some extracts from her letter and from my reply may help others in distress. She wrote:

> I have been so utterly lost in the depths of misery I just haven't known what to say. Somehow I just could not find the words, I'm in such a bleakness of spirit at the moment.
>
> No doubt it will eventually pass from me, as at present I find myself completely cut off from the grace of God and every source of comfort. Oh, this is an awful thing to have to say to you when I know you've been praying for us. I know it's my fault for not being receptive—but I seem to have lost the will-power to try, and sometimes I just can't help rebelling. As for mummy she says she sometimes feels quite calm and peaceful but sometimes she despairs as badly as ever. I could stand feeling bad myself if only mummy was all right—but I get angry that God makes mummy suffer so much. I know it's silly, but that's what makes me feel bitter. Oh, I suppose I'm expecting too much too soon. Anyway, that's what it's really like under the superficial fact that we all appear to have got over it quite well.
>
> Oh, Miss Ikin, I hadn't meant to write all this and let you

know how bitter and miserable I am, but somehow, once I'd started I could not help myself. I don't think I can put on a false front to you.

Do please forgive me for having burdened you with all this—but it's a relief to get it off my chest: and in spite of all this I somehow can't be entirely pessimistic—even though God seems to have forsaken me (or is it the other way round?). I feel that perhaps it won't always be so, and perhaps this is the darkness one must go through before one reaches the light.

This poignant letter shows the impact of the shock of bereavement on someone brought up in a Christian home, who finds her faith challenged by it. My reply to this *cri du cœur* may help others to win through distressing experiences to a deeper faith that has weathered a storm which at first threatened to destroy it.

Some extracts from my reply ran as follows:

My dear Maude,

I am very glad you feel you can't put on a false "front" with me and could tell me just how bad you felt inside. It is true that even those who love us rarely know how we really feel in some tragic set of circumstances unless they themselves have been through something similar which knocked the bottom out of their world. Only then did they find the underlying foundations in God's world that cannot ultimately be destroyed by anything that happens in time.

When all goes well we tend to think the sun will always shine. Yet while it is shining for us, others are suffering. It is no use pretending one isn't feeling bitter about it, if for the time being one is. It is far better to tell God you think He's made a bad mess of things for such suffering to come either to oneself, or to those we love, if you feel like that, than to be "resigned" to it as the Will of God to be accepted. It is *not* the will of God in any direct sense. I am sure God does not "will accidents". But He has made a world in which good will, co-operation, intelligence and responsibility produce results far beyond what anyone could achieve alone. But that being so, the results of sins, negligences and ignorances, of selfishness, unco-operativeness, stupidity and irresponsibility *must* be allowed to bring suffering and disaster, or we could never act responsibly and intelligently or do anything for anyone else at all.

These consequences, like the good fortune of being born in a happy, comfortable home and not in a slum tenement, do fall on us apart from our own deserts or faults respectively. We all share in the entail of both good and evil. So tragedies do happen, accidents do occur, which make us realise how much we had taken our previous good fortune for granted. Yet the benefits we enjoyed had depended on the work of millions of people, in past ages as well as today.

In a personal tragedy, when the dark side of life seems to press us down, we have a chance either to squander the spiritual capital of the ages, or to add to it by our own, surmounting the disaster in such a way that ultimately we find we have gained *something that is really won from life, which is our own, and not a second-hand faith.* If we can do so we find this is worth the price paid for it and is greater than what we seemed to have lost. There is no short cut or easy way to that: nor do all win through to it. But it is always a possibility hidden within tragedy. The good in the long run is stronger than evil. It is creative, whereas evil is destructive and cannot survive indefinitely.

I think it helps us if instead of thinking of God as making one suffer (or as you say "making mummy suffer") we realise the truth that He cared enough to come right down *into* the suffering caused by the cumulative sins and selfishness of all. In Gethsemane He really shared it and found the burden intolerable. Again on Calvary He cried out: "My God, my God, why hast thou forsaken me?" before He could say, "It is finished, into Thy hands I commend my spirit". This meant that He realised that in the long run He could bring us through whatever suffering we encounter in life, into a fullness of the life that has triumphed over the worst that could happen to it. This life, the resurrection life, is beyond being distorted again by evil, since that has done its worst without destroying it.

The resurrection life was not something magically imparted from above the conflict. It was won for us through the actual transformation of the worst concentration of evil that malice could inflict, into the sign and guarantee of victory, through a power of love greater than all we run into in the process of growing up into the Kingdom of Heaven.

When we realise God is not inflicting the suffering, either as punishment or callously, but is sharing it, and that He is active in all the goodwill and desire to help that is evoked in others by our need, our bitterness goes and we begin to find His way through to the best that is possible.

Always be honest with God, dear.[1] If you want to blame Him when things press too heavily, do so. He'll understand and it is far better than a pretence God, to whom you can only speak in your politest tones. You will find, if you really do protest if something seems hard and unfair, He'll answer by bringing something you have left out of account into your mind, either directly or through someone else (cf. my letter which *is* the response to your courage in saying what you really felt), until the angry bitterness has gone and you can begin to realise there is a Power *that can transform our worst feelings* if we will only bring them into relation with Him, and not just our happy feelings or pious hopes. I think of one very real prayer sent up in a moment of emergency by a man exasperated beyond endurance, "Help me, God. I want to wring her b . . . . neck!" God can answer prayers like that when He can't answer abstract ones to "make us good" in general. True prayer has to be learnt in life, not just in Church.

So take heart, Maude, and trust your mother to win through too. Help her to carry *her* burden: but don't try to carry it for her."

Some of you may be surprised, perhaps even shocked, at the temerity of encouraging anyone to blame God. This is not to be taken as general advice! It is only when feelings have raised an otherwise impassable barrier between the individual and his or her *conception* of God that blaming Him can break down the barrier and enable the *real* love of God to reach us and bring peace. Our normal response to the sense of His Presence is worship, trust, awe or love. But my young friend had been feeling angry with God for, as she thought, causing so much suffering, and her anger had made her feel cut off *from* Him, though she had not herself seen the connection between the two.

Some time after this I came across an example quoted by Dr. Christopher Woodard which makes the same point.

A mother had been told her boy was a victim of an incurable and malignant disease. Everything that could be done medically was being done. Then, as she said, "The climax came, as I knew it would, when he was discharged from hospital

[1] It is actually much harder really to be honest with God than most people realise. It demands an honesty and sincerity in ourselves which is not easily come by. Often only great stress brings us to it and to a newness of life as a result.

with these instructions: 'You must bring him up for examination once a month, and as the more advanced symptoms show themselves we will have him back for further treatment.' It was this grim future that completely crushed my spirit. It was no use, I could not face it, and I resolved to end everything. There was nothing left to live for.

"Having made this decision I went into the garden one morning, and although I have always loathed to hear bad language, even in its mildest form, yet at the very top of my voice I called God every bad word I knew. My poor husband, himself driven to distraction with the worry of the past few weeks, added to which was now the worry that my mental condition was rapidly deteriorating, put his hand over my mouth, and implored me to pull myself together. I tore his hand away and shouted, 'What does it matter, what does anything matter any more? There isn't even a God, and so I can do no harm; and if there is a God I am already in Hell. I cannot possibly suffer any more, and I'll give Him a jolly good run for His money.'

"Oh yes, you might well be shocked, but now I will make a very bold statement. I feel certain that it was at this moment that Jesus looked down on me with compassion. 'Father, forgive her,' He said, 'for she knoweth not what she is saying.' For the first time in my life I was being honest with God. I was telling Him what I really thought of Him, and I meant every word I said. The memory of that tragic morning will remain with me for ever, and will always fill me with humiliation and shame; but the more I think of it, the more I look upon this episode as the crisis in God's pattern. In the past I, too, had dressed up in my best with all the frills and furbelows, and attended church: had sung the Venite, Exultemus Domino and the Psalms as lustily as anybody: I, too, had prayed—and that was when I was full of sin, not when I was blaspheming God. Although I had sung songs of praise to God on high, had I ever given a thought to the meaning of the words? No, I was much too busy singing. And those prayers with the responses just tumbling out of my mouth parrot-fashion, did they mean anything? Again I say, no. I was much too busy praying."[1]

The woman tells how she started to read a book which a friend left, and could not leave it until it was finished. The outcome of it was that she visited the author, Dr. Woodard. She goes on to say, "That first visit to him is something very precious to me, and I can only say that I left his room an entirely different person. I am being absolutely honest when I say that my care was left behind in his consulting room, and I was free and quite willing that God should have Peter. I knew Peter would be perfectly safe with Him."[2]

But the sequel to this was the recovery of Peter! When we honour God by being *really* honest with Him, even if that means pouring out the accumulated bitterness of a lifetime on Him, God *can* and *does* respond by removing the causes of the bitterness in ourselves, and in time in our outward circumstances too.

It seemed more than a coincidence that I should come across this after having advised someone to let off her anger, bitterness and resentments against God as forcibly as she could. The grounds for my faith in this unorthodox advice are personal, as may be guessed. I doubt if anyone could rightly give it or speak so without presumption if they had not found a similar turning point in their own lives. But when one has "touched bottom" and found God was there, one may sometimes help another to find the way through the depths of his own particular "false bottom", to the Rock underneath. But it is a searching way. Honesty with oneself is not easy to come by. We all put up a façade like the woman too busy singing to discern the meaning, too busy letting the responses tumble out correctly to realise *her prayers were not reaching their mark.* The very forms of religion can become a barrier between ourselves and God and only some deep crisis in our personal life reveals the sham and makes it possible for reality to break through.

[1] *A Doctor's Faith Holds Fast*, pp. 34–5. [2] Ibid., p. 37.

In Dr. Woodard's next book, however (*A Doctor's Faith is Challenged*), he goes on to say that though Peter recovered sufficiently to go back to school and all were expecting his progress to be maintained, yet he died. He then shows how real a victory was won through apparent defeat. Peter's mother's own words on the day of the funeral will help all other mothers. She writes: "It is just over two years ago that Peter became gravely ill, and my husband and I were told that no medical skill could save our boy. We did the one and only thing possible: we surrendered him wholly into the hands of God, believing implicitly, as I still do, that Christ *can* heal all manner of sickness as much to-day as two thousand years ago. With this in mind and with absolute trust in God, Canon Hughes, Dr. Woodard, and myself and numerous friends put up a terrific battle for Peter's complete recovery.

"The outcome was not as anticipated and outwardly we have lost the fight, but my faith remains unshaken. We could so easily feel as Christ's disciples must have felt on the evening of that first Good Friday: was the fight in vain? Was our 'experiment'—if such it may appear to many—a failure after all? Without the slightest hesitation I can honestly say, 'No, never!' To me it will always be a triumphant victory.

"A healing miracle did take place: but it was on me that this blessing was bestowed. God gave me courage. The last two years with Peter have been the happiest in my life and during this period God has revealed wonderful truths. . . .[1]

"What a long road I have travelled with Peter! All my doubts and prejudices regarding the unknown and the unseen have completely vanished and in their place a true knowledge of the love of God exists. I could no more live without His Presence now than I could live without food. I feel as if I had been born again into a new world, where life is real and full of beauty and where my heart wants to sing all day long."[2]

Dr. Woodard goes on to say: "What perhaps was the most

[1] Pages 51, 52. [2] Page 55.

wonderful thing of all was Peter's own confidence and trust right to the last moment. He knew the presence of Jesus throughout his illness in a way few human beings are privileged to know it. Truly this was not failure but supreme victory."[1]

Peter's mother's inner victory is perhaps shown supremely on the night of Peter's funeral in the last of her words quoted by Dr. Woodard.[2] "There, in the still of the evening, underneath a starlit sky, I offered my heart to God, and as I stood in silent prayer, on the very spot where just two years before, almost to the very day, I had cursed God so bitterly with all the hate and resentment possible, I heard, deep down within me, a gentle voice say 'Susan, mother of Peter, lovest thou me?' And with tears streaming down my face I whispered 'Lord, Thou knowest all things, Thou knowest that I love Thee'."

This is indeed a true Victory over Suffering.

[1] Page 59. [2] Page 59.

## III

# BREAK OUT, BREAK DOWN OR BREAK THROUGH?

IN "EVERYMAN'S MISSION"[1] DR. REBECCA BEARD REFERRED TO "Crisis" in Chinese as made up of two characters: one of which stands for disaster and the other for opportunity. We should do well to heed this. So often we think of crisis as only disastrous. Yet within each crisis is an opportunity that may be brought out of potentiality into actuality. Break out, break down or break through are equally live options in emergencies.

To quote Dr. Beard once more, crises represent extremes of tension. The waves of the ocean rise to their crest, then fall back into a trough. After these peaks and dips of ultimate position, a complete reversal must be made. At the point of highest tension an explosion takes place with a tremendous release of energy.

"Years ago," she goes on, "Thomas Troward, the great English metaphysician, compared the crises in an individual life to the octave. We go through a full octave of experience until we reach the last note. That note becomes either the first note of the higher octave or we drop back to begin the same octave again.

"The individual life is usually made up of smoothly moving cycles. There is seldom anything to show where one cycle ends and another begins until we are challenged by suffering, loss, frustration or deep desire. Then we are drawn out of the orbit of our usual daily activity and brought to a point of

[1] *Everyman's Mission* by Dr. R. Beard is published by Arthur James of Evesham, 10/- post free.

extreme tension from which one of two things must happen—either we go on over into the next step or we drop back into the trough of the wave.

"*If we can move completely through the crises, we pass into a higher dimension of being. If not, we fall back and must repeat the experience.* [Italics mine.] When we come to the zero hour, we can pass through the crisis if we are willing to reduce the resistance of our little self to a minimum by learning the true humility Jesus taught.

"But suppose we reach that climax and the ego in us refuses to die. Some acute disappointment, some deep hurt or tragic loss brings us up to the crest of the wave, but we rebel and fight rather than let go and accept: the ego in us cannot quite give up. Then all of the tremendous energy that is released there at the zenith of tension becomes polarised in the negative and hurls us back into the depths of the trough. Out of the darkness of that reaction come hate and revenge, viciousness and bitterness, and sometimes a cruelty that stupefies us. It is only when we go on over and the little self is really lost that we come out of the spiral into the next dimension. But if we cannot let go of the ego and so lower our resistance, then the release of energy will throw us back upon ourselves, rather than up and over."[1]

### *Break Through*

It may help to quote once more from Rebecca Beard. "When my colleagues said to me 'You are through: put your affairs in order, for you cannot survive another heart attack' I could scarcely believe it, even though the attacks had been terrifying. There was a tenacious hope that I could, by sheer force of will, bring myself out of it. But when they gave me up and I stood alone I realised at last that it was going to take something more than my own will-power to pull me through. Besides, my vitality

[1] *Everyman's Mission*, pp. 71, 73, 74.

had been sapped to the point where I no longer, of myself, had the strength or the courage to fight. Where was I to go? Upon what was I to depend?

"There was only one place to go and that was on my knees. I cried out, 'What are you? Where are you? I don't even know what to call you, but come and talk to me. If you are there, help me. Either take me out of this, or send me on.' And because my surrender was complete and my admission of failure absolute, there came a tremendous illumination of Reality. . . . With blinding clarity, I saw that I was part of the life of the universe. I was one with it. It was not a thing apart from me: it was part of me and I was part of it. The words of Jesus came back to me 'I and my Father are one' and I knew what He meant. Out of the crisis and that great illumination I went on over the crest into another dimension—into perfect health and another form of life."[1]

### *Break Out, Break Down or Break Through*

Break Out, Break Down or Break Through illustrates three ways of meeting such crises in personal life. Those who break out are the criminals, the delinquents, the rebels. They identify themselves with the unregenerate natural ego, refusing to transcend it in a wider and fuller life. They break out in anti-social action as the *only way they can see of asserting themselves.*

Those who break down are the neurotics, who with forces more evenly balanced cannot just "break out"; their ideals are too real for that. Yet they cannot accept the incompatibility of the more primitive elements in themselves with their ideals as a challenge to develop them onto a more mature level. So these primitive elements are repressed and act as an internal saboteur, defeating their good intentions. The criminal avoids a civil war

[1] *Everyman's Mission*, pp. 73–4.

within himself at the price of conflict with society. The neurotic is engaged in a civil war within himself which in times of stress renders him useless to himself or society. He may be intelligent and cultured and yet at critical moments he is liable to fall ill. This seems to provide an alibi for something he unconsciously realises to be beyond him. The excuse "If only I'd not fallen ill I could have managed" is a very different reaction from that of Rebecca Beard, who admitted she was at the end of *her* resources, and found in so doing she could draw on those of God.

Daniel Poling, in *Faith is Power*, gives another kind of example.

"Again the enemy opened fire. Again the earth rose in geysers all about us. That was my second bout with stark terror. I had argued with myself that it wasn't my party anyhow, that I wasn't under orders, that I had just volunteered to help. But it was no good. I knew myself for what I was—a coward. Then I prayed! My prayer was an unvoiced shouting agony in my soul. I remember now it was like this: 'God help me not to run again!' And He did help me. I went out and came back again. Until night fell and the danger was past, God kept His promise: and in keeping that promise with me gave other men, perhaps as frightened as I, fortitude to stay it through.

"It is the strength and courage to 'stay through' that one occasion," he goes on, "you and I and every other man and woman find to be the immediate and imperative requirement. No task however humble and no situation however remote from the spectacular are beyond 'His love and care' if it is a task or a situation for which you and I are responsible. The one thing required and all that is required is that we shall 'ask'."[1]

The difference between break out, break down or break through may hinge on that ability to hold out just the few seconds longer to draw on invisible, but very real reinforcements,

[1] *Faith is Power*, pp. 47–9.

which come when the need is real and our commitment to the "job in hand" is sincere enough. This is true whether the crisis is internal or external—and when once we have known in our own experience the reality of such help, we also know it is available for *all* others in like case; though not all reach out to make it their own. Daniel Poling's prayer was truly "In Christ's name". He did not pray to be kept safe from the external danger. He prayed for help not to run out of it again: that was a prayer God could answer. His subsequent record showed how fully his faith was justified in his life. He became President of the World's Christian Endeavour Union. He also represented the Federal Council of Churches of Christ in America, on many missions during the war. In a personal letter to Dr. Poling, President Roosevelt wrote: "Your selection by the Churches of America as their representative makes you, in these significant days, your country's spiritual ambassador of good will. You will become the voice of millions of fellow Christians."[1]

Since personal experience is the only real testimony here, a reference to an experience of my own may perhaps be permitted. After a long night's agony I had felt my self-control going and sent up an agonising prayer, "This is beyond me. You'll *have* to do something, God, and *do it NOW*", and *instantly* the turmoil ceased and a great peace enfolded me. And when the nurse brought my breakfast a few minutes later, she never realised how near to "cracking" I had been.

Later, when I went to see a girl with an abscessed tooth and a face swollen out of all recognition, after three sleepless nights in spite of sedatives, this experience stood me in good stead. I realised she was just at breaking point, almost frantic with pain, and something must be done. I put a hand on her forehead and sent up a silent prayer, "Please use me to help", and *instantly*—again note the "instantly"—I felt her pain was easing and said, "That's better, isn't it, E.?"; and in great surprise she said,

[1] From p. 167 and the dust cover of *Faith is Power* by Daniel A. Poling.

"Yes." Within a few minutes she said, "It doesn't hurt at all now, Miss Ikin, and I think I could go to sleep." So I said I would keep my hand on her head until she was asleep and then slip out. As I prayed silently the swollen face began to resume its more normal contours and in an incredibly short space of time she was sound asleep. She knew nothing of the laying on of hands, and did not even realise I was praying. There was no preparation, just the recognition of an emergency and the SOS for help that of myself I could not give. God is as near and as available as that.

### *Harnessing Our Emotions*

Crises such as the ones quoted are not "norms" but *nodal* points that make transitions possible when mounting tension imperils the wholeness or integrity of the self because some factor—either good or evil—has been left out of account and the friction arising from ignoring that aspect of reality blocks the way. We can train ourselves, or help to train another generation, to avoid these extremes, so that we can rise with the mounting wave and go over the crest with insight (as one can ride through the breakers when swimming) instead of, as so many do, breaking down or breaking out.

World crises are individual crises writ large. War expresses the *break-out*, when peaceful methods of co-operation have failed to take into account the real needs on both sides for some more equitable adjustment. Yet after the break-out, negotiations have to be resumed, with much of value lost in the frenzy of destruction. Yet peace at any price is not the break-through, but the *break-down* of the ideals embodied in a valued way of life. To let them go to save our skins is to lose the possibility of the very way of life we valued. It is significant that to-day peoples and nations are prepared to fight for a "way of life", for the right to live in that way, even at the cost of material goods and many valuable lives. Yet we are all realising that the destructiveness of atomic and hydrogen bombs could destroy the very civilisations each side is anxious to maintain and protect. Neither the "break out" into war, nor the "break down" into appeasement at the cost of real principle can help. The "break through" that can avert war must come from a deeper creative understanding of the conflicting forces on *both* sides. It needs a widening of the area of effective co-operation in the practical issues that affect the lives and interests of *all* peoples.

God has shown us in unmistakable terms that mankind, with all its rich diversity, is ONE, and that unless we can learn to "love our neighbour as one like ourselves", neither we nor our neighbours may survive the holocaust that would follow a third break-out of global war within a century.

Yet the very magnitude of the challenge may stimulate the creative spiritual forces within mankind to tackle the problem of preventing war as a means of settling international disputes. This may create, through its travail, the very organs for effective co-operation in fighting all that hinders *the true development of man.*

For a short time after the First World War there was a possibility the second might have been prevented: but the War to end War did not end the tensions and conflicts in the souls of men and a second, and worse, outbreak occurred. Can we learn through the consequences of this how to prevent a third, and still worse, war? We have got to learn *how* to live together, if we are to continue to live at all in a world that brings those of all nations into such close contact through radio, press, television and air travel. Scientific knowledge is not the monopoly of a "favoured people", but a glimpse into the way God has made things to work in the world in which He has set us.

Rebecca Beard's vivid picture of rising to the crest of the wave and either going on over it with the impetus of the rising tide behind us, or falling back into the trough, is relevant. If we fail to rise to it the experience, with all its suffering, is repeated until a fresh crisis presents us with another opportunity. This goes on until we find the right way through onto the fresh level that can set us free from the vicious circle that had been bound by the past.

Emotions are the great driving power within us. If these can be harnessed constructively, we can face our crises, individually and nationally, with a great tide of life to carry us forward. If, on the other hand, we are bogged down in negative emotions, concerned with our wrongs, then not only is our inner state that of the hell of someone too entangled to see the light of God's pattern and purpose of love, but such energies become literally destructive.

We see this in family quarrels, class wars, civil wars and war amongst the nations, in which so much of real value in all classes and nations is destroyed. We can only see what is actually wrong in some situation in its true perspective when we are more concerned with discovering and maintaining what is right in the total situation. We can then deal with the real wrong or injustice *practically* instead of *emotionally*. Such conflicts internally, within individuals, may also produce psychosomatic disease.

### *Psychosomatic Disease*

One of the most encouraging signs that there is the possibility of a break-through onto a more mature creative level of life is the development of psychosomatic medicine from the scientific side, and the recognition of the emotional factors crippling our living amongst those applying spiritual therapy to those who are physically, psychologically or spiritually sick.

Psychosomatic diseases are caused by the persistence of emotional reactions which throw the delicate balance of our normal physiological functions out of gear and, by excess or defect of some secretion, put undue strain on the total resources of our strange body-mind-spirit nature. This sets up a vicious circle that needs skilled outside help to cure. All the negative emotions, if maintained and held in the mind, are destructive and all-round capacity is greatly reduced. Hospitals are full of patients whose greatest need is not just the restoration of physical function but the discovery of a new attitude to life, a new way of meeting its challenges. It is here that psychological medicine and spiritual therapy overlap. Medicine alone cannot effect a permanent cure, though it may be essential at some stages to give the personality another chance to gather its resources together and try again. This needs to be combined with help to understand how this came about and loving care in the long process of re-education.

In *Religion and Psychotherapy*, written in 1935, I predicted there would be a great increase in mental and nervous disorders within the next twenty or twenty-five years.[1] I also predicted that in the process of tackling the problem on so wide a scale a deeper understanding of the many factors, quite beyond the control of the particular individuals who succumbed, would be gained which would in time lead to effective methods of prevention. After reaching a peak I then foresaw the possibility of a steady decline in the percentage of those who broke down in this way. Children would be given a better start in stabilising their emotional life so as to grow towards a happy maturity. In addition those needing help at critical transitional stages would be able to get more of the necessary psychological and spiritual help to enable them, too, to win through to a fuller life than would have seemed possible to sufferers written off as the "chronics" of a generation ago.

## *Emotional Factors in Accidents*

Some accidents do happen independently of our emotional life. A gale that rips off a chimney-pot and hurls it on to the

[1] This prediction has been confirmed. More than half the beds in hospitals in the U.S.A. are said to be filled with sufferers from psychosomatic diseases. A large proportion of those in our own hospitals likewise need psychological and spiritual therapy, as well as medical attention and care.

head of a passer-by is not caused by any emotion within that individual, although some individuals might be alert enough to dodge it, or intuitive enough to sense impending disaster and side-step it. But this would not apply when whole buildings are blown down, a train crashes, an earthquake or a tornado sweeps all before it.

As we have seen in "Why Do the Innocent Suffer?" accidents are the price paid for sufficient reliability and stability in our surroundings for us to rely upon the abiding consequences of real, definite and predictable sequences of events.

Nevertheless, emotional factors do play a large part in accidents that involve human agency at some stage in the sequence. Contrary to what might be expected to be evenly distributed, it is found that some people rarely have an accident while others seem to be involved in one after another. The latter are called "accident prone" and emotional factors are found to be largely responsible for this. The fine co-ordination of mental and physical capacities in skilled action depends on the efficiency of the whole system. An emotional upset disturbs this and the reactions of a driver, for example, may be slower in an emergency, and before he has time to think the accident has occurred and he, or someone else, may be badly injured as a result. So, too, in the home, after a quarrel, a woman may knock over a kettle of boiling water and get severely scalded, without realising this was the direct result of disturbed emotions which prevented the automatic muscular control which would have lifted the kettle off in safety. Crockery, likewise, seems to "slip through our fingers" if we are upset. Most of us will have some experience of the truth of this, if we are honest with ourselves when things go wrong. The days when one thing after another seem to go wrong often start with some small thing which threw us off balance. The results of that increased our lack of poise, until a crescendo of minor mishaps may cause us to see what is wrong with *ourselves* for *things* to be so awkward. The moment we stop blaming anything outside ourselves for something that is within us, the situation changes and even inanimate things seem to be responsive and amenable to our purposes and work gets done in half the time.

Getting the best out of ourselves, the best out of other people and the best out of the material environment go together. If we seem to get more than our fair share of the accidents or "downs" of life, it will pay us to take stock of our inner attitude *to* life. It isn't always easy to accept the fact that our own attitude has precipitated or attracted to us many of the negative conditions with which we are struggling: nor, if this is seen, to avoid feeling paralysed by the responsibility. Yet if we can face it responsibly, the tide can turn. Though none of us can be immune, as we have seen, from the effects of the "sins, negligences and ignorances" of others, we can increasingly avoid the ills that come from blaming them when our own are involved. Accident proneness involves a deep-seated insecurity in life. This may superficially seem to be caused by the external mishaps. A deeper insight, however, shows they have resulted from the insecurity and inferiority which prevented the mastery of either the self or its tools. To realise this is to take a real step towards a better future, not only for the individual, but for all connected with him.

The necessity for dealing with both psychosomatic diseases and the emotional causes of accidents, has led to the need for further education to prevent much of this all too human cause of suffering.

### *A Way Through*

The provision of Child Guidance Clinics and the opening of the doors of mental hospitals to "voluntary patients", instead of waiting till they had forcibly to be detained through becoming dangerous to themselves or others, are two big steps in the right direction. Marriage Guidance counselling will help many more to steer through the difficulties that arise through emotional immaturities that prevent the full happiness of married life being experienced. This in its turn will help children of the next generation to get a better start.

Pastoral counselling, too, has greatly increased in its range and scope. This has a very real part to play, as we find amongst the many cases of psycho-neurotic, or psychosomatic disorders, a sense of guilt plays a big part.

The revival of the Church's Ministry of Healing and increased awareness of spiritual factors in life and health is bringing hope of cure to many through the realisation that God is on the side of health. We are only on the fringe of all the possibilities this opens out.

Health is positive: sickness is negative. Man is made to function physically through his body, mentally through his mind and spiritually through his spirit or soul. When these three are in harmony he enjoys positive health and is able to resist disease. Sickness results when this harmony breaks down on any of these levels. Because man is a unity, this affects the total functioning of his life and personality. Symptoms may appear to be physical as a result of mental and spiritual conflict. The real level of disease is not always what it seems.

Where sickness produces growths, surgeons can operate. Where there are certain deficiencies such as vitamins, or essential minerals, the medical profession can replace these. In some cases this lack is purely physical. Rickets due to lack of calcium, scurvy due to a lack of vitamin C, and beri-beri due to a lack of vitamin B are examples of these. But in others, even with adequate supplies in their food, some internal factor prevents their assimilation. Psychiatrists seek to find the causes of disharmony within the mind, and, as has been shown, emotional factors play a part in many disorders of the body.

But man is more than his body or his emotions. He is also more than his mind. *There is at the centre of our real being a point of contact with a world of spirit which transcends the space and time within which our minds and bodies function.* Man is only truly and fully himself when this is in harmony with the mental and physical laws which give rise to healthy mental and physical functioning on earth. Surgeons can operate, doctors can replace certain deficiencies and psychiatrists can probe the mind. But true healing comes from God through this hidden spiritual centre of our being. Doctors may call it Nature: but God is more than nature left to itself.

In man's fight for victory over suffering all three parts or levels of his being should receive equal attention. There is a science of physical functioning—physiology. There is a science of mental functioning—psychology. But there is no adequate or agreed science of spiritual processes,[1] *which are even more fundamental for man's welfare*. Yet it is within this sphere, I am convinced, that ultimate healing for body, mind and spirit must come.

All real healing comes from God. He has made provision in our bodies for coping with invasions by disease germs. He has made provision for the rapid repair of tissues damaged by accident in a way no machine can repair itself. If the injury is too serious for this, He takes us out of the crippled body by death. He has made provision in our minds for compensatory activities to adjust disharmony and imbalance. Otherwise no one could have survived the experiences of the last fifty years. Of recent years, our minds have held such extremes of brutality, despair, broken hopes and faith. Yet they have also given rise to heights of heroism, and to much effort to relieve and heal the sufferers and refugees, who are still paying so high a price for the failure of the civilising factors in experience to avert the disaster. The urgency of the situation and its widespread nature may in time lead us to try to find a better way of life.

God has also made provision for awareness of and response to Himself. This is His greatest gift to man. But it is also man's greatest danger. The response to God must be a free one, a real

[1] The title of *pneumiatrist* has been coined by some workers in America to distinguish what they call their spiritual therapy from that of the secular *psychiatrist*. (Pneuma=Spirit. Psycho=Mind.)

one: not one imposed or enforced by God. It is one He makes possible and we have to make it actual.

Wherever we fail to do so we distort our nature and evils multiply. As we have seen in the suffering of the innocent, this does affect others. Moreover, each wrong choice makes it harder to respond aright to the next opportunity God gives to bring us back into harmony with Himself. The cumulative effects of millions of failures to respond to God aright is responsible for the evils in the world, with which *all* of us have to cope. The climax of this on Calvary, when the full burden on Christ Incarnate was borne *voluntarily*[1] to bring men back freely to the way of God, was God's way of showing His love would never leave us to bear the consequences of sin alone. By themselves the consequences of sin harden the sinner and cut him off from the Divine help he can only appropriate or respond to willingly. The consequences of sin borne by Christ freely can evoke a response in the heart of the sinner that no despotic God could do by over-ruling our wayward wills by force.

This is the central fact at the root of all truly spiritual healing. Christ's redeeming work involves a genuine reversal of man's self-centred way of life. This reversal restores harmony between man and His Creator (Father). The descending spiral into one disaster after another, changes into the ascending spiral of the return to Our Father's home and standards of living. This forgiving welcome is always something we realise is a free gift of God. It is not a privilege that is deserved or earned. It is not our own righteousness that saves us: but a love that will not let us go until He *has* blessed us, however much suffering to ourselves or others this may involve. *Christ does break the entail of evil.* The very consequences, as we have seen, can bring out

[1] The emphasis on willingness may at first sight seem inaccurate, since the ecclesiastical powers of the day had determined to make away with One who threatened their prestige. But it was the ability to go forward to His death instead of running away and evading the consequence of the challenge of His way of life, in order to fulfil the Father's will, that made resurrection possible. His life and death are tied together spiritually.

deeper spiritual resources in those who have found freedom in Christ from the vicious circle of entanglement in themselves than could ever have been foreseen.

### *Flexibility and Vigilance*

The combination of flexibility and vigilance is the key to the break-through dynamically and creatively out of situations, whether internal or external, which otherwise can issue disastrously in break-outs or break-downs. We need flexibility to let less mature reactions go as soon as we sense the pull or call of Christ within us. We need vigilance not to miss this. We also need to be alert to *all* sources of help available to us at critical points in the crises of life which embrace danger and opportunity alike.

It is many years since I wrote, "If there are twenty-nine ways of going right and only one way of going wrong, the man who always expects things to go wrong will surely find that one way of making them do so. If there are twenty-nine ways of going wrong, and only one way of going right, the man who is genuinely seeking the right way will find the one way that does avert disaster."

> "One ship drives east, another drives west
> While the self same breezes blow;
> 'Tis the set of the sail and not the gale
> That bids them where to go.
>
> Like the winds of the sea are the ways of fate
> As we journey along through life;
> 'Tis the set of the soul that decides the goal
> And not the calm or the strife."[1]

[1] *Rebecca*, by R. Williams.

## IV

# LIFE'S COMMON WAYS

AFTER FACING SOME OF THE MORE TRAGIC ASPECTS OF LIFE, AND finding a clue to guide us through such crises, it is necessary to bring our insights back into life's common ways.

For the majority of folk, earning a living or running a home and bringing up a family is the sphere within which the Holy Spirit must work to bring their lives into harmony and fulfilment. This is an important recognition of the necessity and value of everyday life. It is the vehicle or medium through which the spirit finds expression on earth.

Nevertheless the framework within which the daily round has to be lived is also the concern of God. It is a commonplace that a less efficient individual, provided with good tools and a suitable environment for work, may actually turn out better work than a superior man with inadequate tools and facilities. Theologians and philosophers grapple with the nature of the ultimate background to, or framework of, life, and the nature of the tools available to us through scientific discoveries, as well as through religious experience. This may in time enable man to work more effectively and happily than is often the case at present. But if this is to be so, the theologian, philosopher or scientist must also be "at home" on the level of life as it is *lived*, and not just thought about from an arm-chair, if the man in the street—that is the vast majority of the human race—is to be helped.

It can help in living more fully within the daily round if there is harmony between real thinkers and those who have to apply such insights as are relevant within their daily work. With so many conflicting "ideologies" to-day, each competing for the loyalty of the common man in fascism, communism, socialism, nationalism, and democracy, thinking must be brought to the test of *life*. Yet few realise the range and extent of the power of creative thinking and the part it plays through creative prayer to transform the banal or distracting elements in our daily routine.

"As a man thinketh in his heart, so he is." The man whose head and heart are in harmony can move mountains of difficulty that neither head nor heart can cope with alone. Both are necessary for the fullness of life: the life Christ came to bring more abundantly to those who follow Him.

Creative thinking and creative praying (i.e. praying that does change the outcome of issues that would be worse left to themselves on the natural level) are connected. Effective prayer is not magic. It is not a substitute for our ordinary work, mental or physical: nor is it a compensation for the failure to put it in! Yet it does bring into play a "plus" that goes beyond the range of our own activities, and yet is in some way proportional to them. All who take their prayer life seriously as a real communion with God—the God of all—form a network through which God can make each more sensitive to His call.

Each of us has his own specific point of contact with God, his own "wave-length" of access in prayer, which is unique and irreplaceable by any other. If we are truly centred in the reality of our own being with this wave-length, free from interference by worry, anxiety, self-seeking, we can both receive and transmit messages from and to God. We then find we are also more truly attuned to the actual demands of our environment. This makes us more effective in action.

Each of us can—if we will—provide God with a point of contact in the midst of the conflicts, confusions, rivalries and ups and downs of everyday life. Alone, these can overwhelm us, so that our thoughts tend to go round in vicious circles, getting more involved and hopeless as a result. But if we can train ourselves to seek first that central "pool of silence" at the centre of the whirlpool and let God "think *His* solution into us", we will find some entirely unexpected aspect of the problem comes into mind. We can then see the next step to take. We also find that in the *taking*, confusion and conflict vanish. We are "geared for action", with thinking, feeling and willing harmonised creatively.

This is true if the action is unpleasant or even painful in its nature: not only when a happy issue is immediate. The cessation of conflict about it and the acceptance of the course of action felt to be right in the circumstances, releases power to fulfil it with a *whole* mind and not a distracted or divided one.

The supreme example of this is Christ in Gethsemane. He saw only too clearly where all the evils around Him on so many levels were converging to break Him, to put an end to the physical Life that challenged them. In an agonised struggle He sought to find some easier way, some way of escape that would give Him a chance to continue His active ministry on earth. "Father, if it be possible, let this cup pass."

Then when He was sure, in the very centre of His being, that the complete overthrow of all His hopes for a long active ministry amongst men was the only way of overcoming the opposition of all the vested interests in maintaining the old ways, He ended with, "Nevertheless, not my will, but thine be done."

From that unification of His will with the Father's came the peace and poise that so impressed Pilate, and a silence that rebuked the noisy clamourings of the crowds that cried, "Crucify him." In the very midst of the turmoil and agony of the crucifixion there was that indefinable something that led the penitent thief on a cross beside Him to recognise Him as lord of a real Kingdom and to ask to be included in it. This same inner integrity also led the centurion to say, "Verily this was the Son of God."

Christ's link with the Eternal was so truly related to *all* the temporal circumstances that the gallows of the day, which seemed to mark the triumph of force over love, has become the sign of the victory of love over force. It is now the Triumphant Cross of the Eternal Christ, who rose from an empty tomb—the very substance of His body raised to an imperishable form by His *inner* victory over death.

This is the secret of the power to live creatively in the midst of life's common ways and life's common burdens, with all the ups and downs, the tangled emotional relationships, and the mixed good and evil in our environment and in ourselves. In Christ's victory under our own earthly conditions, in and through the worst that *any* combination of circumstances can produce, we have the surety, the pledge, the guarantee, that God can transform the frustrating circumstances of our lives and take them up within the range of His ultimate victory over all that tries to defeat Him.

In such a faith we continually find Him at work within life's common ways, transforming them and us in proportion to the sincerity of our dedication of them to His service.

Nicoll says, "All that we have done so far may be gathered up into some spiritual existence, into a kind of spiritual sum-total, and all that we are doing now, in what we take as our sole existence, may be effecting and be effected by, this spiritual sum-total of existence."[1] This may well be true.

Life's common ways include highways and byways, rough roads and smooth roads, plain roads and mountain tracks: crowded cities and desert places.

But as John Oxenham says:

"To everyman there openeth
A high way and a low
And everyman decideth
The way his soul shall go.

[1] *Living Time*, p. 179.

The high soul takes the high road,
  The low soul takes the low:
And in between in the misty flats,
  The rest drift to and fro.

But to everyman there openeth
  A high way and a low,
And everyman decideth
  The way his soul shall go."

## V

# GUILT AND FORGIVENESS

IN TRAVELLING THIS ROAD, HOWEVER, SOME DETOURS MAY BRING shame, remorse and guilt, which are all intensely painful emotions. Many of us at times must have felt like the small boy who had accidentally put his knee through the curtain while climbing onto a window seat. He looked at the hole ruefully, and then said, "I wish I was the bigly hole and the bigly hole was me!"

We have seen that negative emotions play a large part in psychosomatic disease, and the many psycho-neurotic conditions that make life seem more like a nightmare than a privilege. Guilt also plays a part in much mental suffering and even in actual mental disease. The medical superintendent of one mental hospital told me they frequently failed to cure patients because they could not deal adequately with their sense of guilt. Another, who was a fellow lecturer with me at a conference of chaplains of mental hospitals, said much of his work consisted in getting rid of his patients' sense of guilt. The bishop who was in the chair said it was difficult to reconcile that with his work, which was to evoke a sense of sin!

Can these apparently opposite sides be reconciled? Yes. Christ said He came to call sinners to repentance, to an awareness of their sin: and then offered the forgiveness that could lift them above it. To the man sick of the palsy He first said, "Son, be of good cheer; thy sins be forgiven thee." In this He was doing what the medical superintendent realised to be necessary, removing the paralysing sense of guilt from a patient. When challenged as to His right to do this Christ said, "Whether it is easier to say, 'Thy sins be forgiven thee'; or to say, 'Take up thy bed and walk'? But that ye may know that the Son of man hath power on earth to forgive sins, (then saith he to the sick of the palsy,) 'Arise, take up thy bed, and go unto thine house.' And he arose, and departed to his house."[1] The sick man realised he could trust and obey the commands of One who had lifted a crushing burden of guilt from his soul.

Yet there is a valid distinction between the need to remove a patient's sense of guilt before healing forces can become active in him and the bishop's aim to evoke a sense of sin. Just because guilt is so painful, our minds use many subterfuges to avoid recognising it. These do need to be stripped away from us if we are to become our real selves—and even a sinful self that recognises itself as such is nearer the Kingdom of Heaven than a proud self-righteous one. The latter by its self-satisfaction makes it impossible to realise there *is* a Kingdom of Heaven beyond the range of its self-limited awareness. Christ's parable of the publican not feeling worthy to lift up his eyes, praying "God be merciful to me, a sinner" and the Pharisee thanking God he was not as other men, has for ever pin-pointed the essential need for humility and sincerity if we would enter the Kingdom of Heaven.

Both doctor and priest may have to help to strip off the disguises with which, when most in need, we tend to hide our real selves. Those who recognise their need can be helped in one way. Those who are not yet aware that they have closed the door to a fuller life, those who are self-satisfied or self-righteous, need to be awakened to their spiritual poverty before they can appreciate the reality of a forgiving love that can redeem them too, and open the way to a life of unending possibilities *if they share it on equal terms with their fellows*.

[1] Matt. 9, vv. 2, 5–7.

### *Guilt and Sin*

Now, perhaps, we are in a position to see a little more clearly the difference between the psychiatrist's work in getting rid of his patient's sense of guilt and the bishop who envisaged his work as evoking a sense of sin.

The kind of guilt the psychiatrist has to remove is a guilt about our actual nature and equipment as human beings. This prevents the full and healthy development of the potentialities in our nature and makes us ashamed of God-given instincts. Where the idea of sex as sinful in itself, for example, has prevented a child's natural curiosity about the origins of life being satisfied objectively, the sense of something unclean is associated with its natural awakening in later life. This makes it more difficult in adolescence, courtship or marriage, to express it appropriately with reverence and delight in the widening world to which it opens the way. A purely "spiritual" love divorced from its means of expression is unreal. Marriage after marriage founders on the split between the physical and spiritual aspects of love and the wholeness the union of *eros* and *agape* can bring.[1]

It is the cumulative effect of guilty feelings associated with natural urges that drives people to "rationalise" their motives. This is the kind of pathological guilt a psychiatrist has to eliminate before any real penitence for sins committed can lead to control and amendment. To try to evoke a sense of sin in someone who has broken down because he already felt too guilty to recognise his real self with its roots in spirit, is to make true insight and recovery still more difficult. It is not only sex impulses that come under this ban of guilt. Aggressiveness and self-assertion also often fall under it. Yet both of these are needed in the growing child to become initiative

[1] This is considered in much more detail in *Sex Problems and Personal Relationships*, jointly written by E. Parkinson Smith and myself. Published by Heinemann.

and endurance in manhood. To crush these as "naughtiness", instead of guiding them into harmony with other attributes within the self, leads to the "break outs" and "break downs" in life. Guilt that is beyond acceptance or endurance is projected onto others, whether these are individuals or nations. These are made into scapegoats to prevent us from facing, and then having to tackle, the roots of evil in ourselves.

The true sense of sin, which is healthy, does not arise through failure to reach an ideal stature out of all relation to capacity, but to a falling below the best that is open to us at each stage. Anyone really living from his own spiritual centre knows the difference between falling short of something it had been within his capacity to have done, for which he rightly feels responsible, and the failure to achieve something into which he had put his best, only to discover that factors outside his control had made success impossible.

We are none of us wholly free and none of us wholly unfree. The range of freedom to do the right, which is the only freedom worth having, increases with every fresh insight into its nature and obedience to its demands on our loyalty. It is restricted by every evasion of our real responsibility: as well as by every attempt to off-shoulder our own part in some quarrel, some accident, or some disharmony onto another. This limits still further our contact with the deeper resources of spirit *in* us, which become available when we really mean business.

The sense of guilt the psychiatrist wishes to remove is a pre-selfconscious guilt that actually paralyses, or prevents, the full maturing of a responsible personality. It also inhibits faith and cuts the individual off from the love he needs both to give and receive by making him feel (and often seem) unlovable.

The sense of guilt is emotional, not fully moral or spiritual. It needs to be outgrown before a true sense of sin, with the responsibility for accepting the consequence of our own actions and intentions, can lead us with genuine penitence to a source of grace that can redeem our twisted lives and restore the "image of

God" in us, and so enable us to love and live freely once more.

This leads us on in the next section to the need for forgiveness and a consideration of some emotions which hinder our capacity to give or receive it.

### *Bitterness or Forgiveness*

Bitterness over some injury is a common difficulty. It is easy to talk glibly of forgiveness when we are happy, well fed and things are going smoothly. It is not so easy when we have suffered, or are suffering, to avoid bitterness creeping in and forgiving love going out. Bitterness and love cannot co-exist. However great or real the injury may have been, to pride, to self-esteem, to our health, livelihood or reputation, it is impossible to see the whole situation truly in perspective while we are actually feeling bitter.

We may say, and think we mean it, that we do forgive the one who has wronged us, misjudged us, or let us down badly. But if bitterness and resentment persist, they show forgiveness is a form, not a reality.

Bitterness and resentment are self-centred emotions which blind us to reality. Forgiveness is other-centred, more concerned with restoring the broken relationship itself than with whose fault it was.

Most of us at some time have found it hard to pray those searching words, "Forgive us our trespasses *as we forgive them that trespass against us.*" That is a boomerang prayer which inevitably recoils on the unforgiving.

U.
10/64

Some time ago when I was feeling really baffled as to how to help someone who was feeling very bitter over the memory of a wrong, a story told me by a mother flashed into my mind. The somewhat harassed mother had asked her ten-year-old daughter to look after her small brother. The girl retorted, "Why should I? He's your child, not mine." I smiled somewhat ruefully, as the recollection slipped into my mind. I was feeling so very much like that ten-year-old girl with regard to the woman I was trying to help. It was taking time and energy that could ill be spared from the work I was doing, and the results did not seem to justify the time and real spiritual effort I'd expended. Yet I could not just "write her off", leaving the wound unhealed. So, like the small girl, I found myself echoing her words in prayer, saying to God, "She's Your child, not mine, why should I carry so much of her burden?"

But the prayer brought its own answer. She was God's child, not mine. I was not responsible for her existence or condition: but I, too, was God's child and had a responsibility to a sister-in-Christ, just as the small girl had one in connection with her brother, who, while not her child, was her brother. Moreover, the reminder that God was ultimately responsible for us both gave fresh hope that He would show how to ease the burden that was issuing in such bitterness.

Bitterness is a sign that some hurt has been greater than could be assimilated spiritually or emotionally, and is unconsciously a heartfelt cry for help, which simultaneously makes it difficult for any real help to get through the barrier it raises.

The impact of the bitterness on anyone seeking to help is painful in two ways. If one is reaching out a helping hand and is therefore *open to the being of another*, the actual contact with the bitterness strikes one almost physically. The natural tendency is to recoil from it and so close the door of compassion in oneself. Yet only in so far as the barriers between selves *are* breached can healing love reach through the bitterness and in some way restore a trust in *life*. The loss of this is more serious than the particular cause of the bitterness itself. Only a love willing to suffer can keep the channel of communication open until the bitterness can be spent and find forgivingness, restoring fellowship in spite of suffering. A mediator is necessary when negative emotions twist and distort everything relevant to the situation. These pile up an increasing barrier which makes mutual understanding more and more difficult to achieve.

The second way the impact of bitterness on a would-be helper is painful, is that the very need to show that bitterness is the sufferer's own reaction to the painful experience tends to draw the bitterness onto the innocent helper with an outburst of "you don't understand". Yet it is necessary to see that this can and must be separated from its external cause. Failure to see this is often followed by the sufferer going off in a huff to hug a double grievance. The bitterness thus infects yet another relationship and so continues to keep love at bay.

Anyone who feels resentful, or bitter, is looking through glasses which distort whatever is seen through them. Argument alone cannot convince them that they are themselves twisting, or exaggerating, whatever has happened, since that is the way in which they perceive and respond to it. The caricature bears some resemblance to the original, just as reflections in distorting mirrors bear some resemblance to the source: but they are so out of proportion and perspective as to be genuinely misleading. Yet until this distortion of vision has been cured, they cannot enter into a direct relation with whomever they are blaming. They only meet the reflection of their own image, so the vicious circle of recriminations continues.

### *Negative and Positive Emotions*

Yet experience is "what happens to us plus our reaction to it". We can't alter the happenings, but we can change our reactions to them when these are inappropriate, exaggerated or upset our balance. Negative emotions, responsible for so much of the suffering and illness in the world, are all self-centred ones. They are reactions to what has happened, however they may seem to be caused by the external happenings that precipitate them. Bitterness expresses a long brooding over a wrong which makes life even more depressing. Positive emotions, on the other hand, are all out-going ones, making contact with others, and with life. They expand the real spiritual self in a true fellowship.

Professor Glenn Clark wrote, "If you are ever asked to pray for a person's health, you will learn, as I have learned, the futility of your prayer unless the one for whom you pray co-operates in removing the life-destroying emotions that prevent the healing power of God from entering. If there are any hates or bitternesses, they must first be cast out before love can come in. If there are any fears, depressions, worries, glooms, they must first be removed before joy can come in. Love and joy are the two greatest healing forces known to man. But you cannot buy these at the chemist's." He goes on, "There can be no permanent health where love is not. But joy is the dynamic flowing power that carries this healing love to others."[1]

Bitterness closes us in on ourselves, on a very sick-and-sorry-for-itself self. Joy is the opening of ourselves to all the creative forces in the universe, whatever our actual immediate circumstances may be.

### *Forgivingness*

We are deeply moved by the story of the airman who lost a leg and whose face and hands were burnt and scarred for life. Someone said, "What a tragic loss." He replied, "It is not a loss, I *gave* it." That example may rebuke our bitterness at some lesser loss. If we can only see through it to the love that made us vulnerable, the bitterness can be changed to a thankfulness that we had cared enough to be hurt. Though still hurt, the door of compassion is open to us. As the bitterness drops out our spiritual eyes are cleared and we see the hurt in truer proportion against the wider background of life and take fresh heart for the future, in spite of a heartache. *Forgivingness sets us free from a life-destroying concentration on ourselves and opens the way for healing and forgiveness to reach us too. It sets divine love circulating once more.*

[1] *I Will Lift Up Mine Eyes*. p. 154. Publishers: Arthur James, Evesham. 11/- post free.

### *Redemptive Love*

A woman recently told me her life had been shattered by finding her husband had been attracted by, and was going with, a younger woman. She, like many another, had trusted her husband implicitly and shared his struggles to win a position and make a home, and had been happy in his love. But the discovery that this infatuation had been going on for some months without her knowledge had shaken her faith in him as well as dealing a blow at her self-confidence. The man had severed his connection with the girl, and they were trying to pick up the threads of married life that had so nearly foundered.

The wife felt she was trying vainly to get back to the halcyon days before this had happened. The memory of what had been going on *before* she realised it, however, made her distrust not only the man but herself. How could she *ever* be sure of him again, she asked.

I tried to show her that it was impossible to get back to the old days: but that in time, by living and working together to make a fresh start *in spite of* what had happened, they might win through eventually to a deeper relationship. Many other married couples have done this when a temporary attraction had seduced a man from his allegiance to a wife whom he had begun to take for granted as a background to his life, instead of the centre of his home.

This, however, I said, depended on the faithfulness of the woman who had been so deeply hurt, and on her willingness not to condone the weakness in the man (which had shown in other directions too) but to recognise and live with it until the new bond was forged. By so doing, I said, though the way might be long and hard, especially while she could not be sure he meant what he said, it might save the man from his own weakness, and the time could come when she would *know* he cared for her again, able once more to trust his love and her own judgement.

As this was said she responded with, "If that happened, if I could really trust him again, then the suffering would have been worth while." So it became possible to say, "That is the kind of love that is redemptive, not seeking for what it can get but holding on through its own betrayal to the one who has betrayed until a new relationship is forged.

"Calvary didn't happen just once 2,000 years ago," I went on. "The redemptive love that was expressed in it by the Christ who forgave His crucifiers could still reinforce our own efforts to forgive those who had hurt us. It could change the natural love of man and wife that had failed to hold into a redemptive love that could heal the scars and deepen the relationship. But," I added, "there is no short cut. It has to be lived out and through: God be with you in the living."

### *The Forgiving Love of Christ*

Christ's love for us is no sentimental love. He could weep over Jerusalem saying, "O Jerusalem, Jerusalem, thou that killest the prophets, and stonest them which are sent unto thee. How often would I have gathered thy children together, even as a hen gathereth her chickens under her wings, and ye would not! Behold your house is left unto you desolate."[1] And of the building of the temple He said, "See ye not all these things? Verily I say unto you, there shall not be left here one stone upon another, that shall not be thrown down."[2]

Yet in His deep compassion He could challenge the accusers of the woman taken in adultery who wanted to stone her, saying, "He that is without sin among you, let him first cast a stone at her." One by one in the face of that searching challenge they slunk out until Jesus and the woman were left alone. He said, "Woman, where are those thine accusers? Hath no man condemned thee?" and she replied, "No man, Lord." "Neither do I condemn thee. Go thy way: from henceforth sin no more."[3]

[1] Matt. 23, vv. 37–8. [2] Matt. 24, v. 2. [3] John 8, vv. 7, 10 and 11.

Christ is calling us to a way of life. He is prepared to forgive our falling short of it, unto seventy times seven, if need be: but He will not let us rest content with less than His way of life, however much suffering may be involved in the transformation. His grace is available for all that is needed at every stage in the transformation from children of nature to children of grace, consciously realising and rejoicing in our spiritual heritage. Sin is our refusal of this grace: or of the channel through which He wishes it to reach us. It is our preference for the time being, for our own way, not His. He will not force His will on us. He lets us go our own way till its consequences bring us to our knees; but the moment we ask His help, it is there.

St. Paul could rightly say, "Where sin did abound, there did Grace yet more abound. Shall we then continue in sin that Grace may abound; God forbid."

No one who realises the cost of forgiving love keeping contact with the sin that is alienating it can ever lightly take that forgiveness or continue in the sin that made it an agony to forgive. It is only through the love that will not let us go, in spite of the agony the betrayal of such love—whatever form it may take—inflicts on the innocent, that a change of heart in the sinful can be effected.

We may repent of sin, we may wallow in remorse, and yet still be bound in the circle of our own self-centredness, unable to take a step outside it. Love has to take us in within the radius of real relationship. Love alone can restore a fellowship sin has forfeited. We can have no rights to a relationship we have spurned. Its restoration must come from beyond ourselves. Our part can only be that of wondering awe and acceptance of a forgiveness we could never have earned, and yet without which we realise we are bankrupt and our natural life just dust and ashes.

Churchill could say after the Battle of Britain, "Never before have so many owed so much to so few." The lives of the many of us who have survived have been "bought at a price". Do we remember that, and seek to repay a fraction of our debt by living so that the freedom for which they gave their young lives may not be thrown away?

Yet just once before in the history of mankind the many owed even more to the few. We were "bought at a price" on Calvary by *One who kept the central citadel of the image of God in man undefiled, and free from sin through the onslaughts of the evil in the universe on every level of His Being*. So through that one centre the Infinite and Eternal love of God can reach through to redeem and to re-create its distorted form in the rest of us.

From the first fruits of that in the small band of His disciples, who had previously fled and left Him to face His destiny alone, millions have been led to the deep springs of life in Christ. The disciples became transformed, able to live and give their own lives fully and freely to witness to the miracle of the resurrection of a Christ whose Spirit they now found in themselves "after the Holy Ghost had come upon them". On the faithfulness of those few in an alien antagonistic world, Christ trusted the extension of the fruits of His sacrifice in ever-widening circles. We are "bought with a price", not only, though supremely, by the love of Christ, but by the lives and love of His followers who made it possible for us to know the "source of our salvation".

In this the Mystery of Suffering reaches its climax. It is the mystery of life through death, of joy through pain triumphantly transcended, of a supreme fellowship won in apparent isolation. It holds within it the agonies and mysteries of all the tears throughout the ages. Calvary is the supreme blot in the universe, the utmost fling of evil. Yet it is also the focal point for the unlimited resources of Infinite love to radiate through to all on whom even the fringe of the shadow of evil presses hard, until in the end all shadows are dispersed, redeemed by that Creative love that nothing can destroy.

# VI

# GUIDANCE IN LIVING

In leading us to full awareness of this divine love at the heart of life God has many ways of guiding us, not all of which we recognise as coming from Him. Many of these we may not even recognise as guidance for living at all, since the guidance comes in the living. It is not just in prayer or in some command given in words that God speaks to us; though, as we shall see later, we can train ourselves—or be trained—to discern His will through a still small voice within. But first we need to discover what we might call the routine ways through which God guides our actions in the world in which we live, and not just our feelings in our devotional life. God is concerned with the whole of life in this amazingly intricate and wonderful world.

### *Guidance through Intelligence*

Professor Kohler has done a great deal of experimental work in connection with the intelligence of chimpanzees. He found that if he tied a chimpanzee to a post with a rope forming only three loops the chimpanzee could see how to disentangle himself, but that if tied with more than three loops it apparently looked an inextricable tangle. The chimpanzee then pulled first one way and then another, frequently getting more entangled in the process. Lest we should think this implied a very low level of intelligence, Professor Kohler suggested we should consider how many of us found a deck chair offered a similar tangle, only to be adjusted by trying first this way and then that, until, often more by good luck than good management, the chair was at last set up.

When either a chimpanzee or a human being can see *how* to do some particular thing, instead of groping blindly until by trial and error he finds the right way, he is using intelligence, and his actions are "guided" by intelligent insight. This is true in spite of a great range in the simplicity or complexity of the action required, and in the capacity of an individual to assess rightly the relations between the various circumstances (in the above case the number of loops to be unravelled) to be altered in order to achieve the desired end.

The Mind of God is an Infinite Intelligence which holds *all* the complicated inter-relations within the universe clearly together and foresees all the possible consequences of actions within it.

This includes suffering due to divergences from the true nature or function of any created elements within the whole, as well as the joy of harmony which accompanies the right relationship of any part within the whole, both to God and its neighbours. So if, in our small way, we can see how to act intelligently within the range of our actual responsibility so that the results we want follow, God is guiding us in the world of action. Whereas if we try to force a way through blindly by sheer will-power, we set in motion a "won't" power that nullifies our efforts.

### *Guidance through Circumstance*

God also guides us through external circumstances, both frustrating and helpful. The man who does not accept the guidance of circumstances will not get very far in life. If, for example, when it is raining heavily a farmer says, "I am going to get my hay in to-day, wet or fine, because I planned to do so", he has only his obstinacy to blame when his crop rots through being stored when it is damp: or when he loses it through fire, since the internal heat of a stack of damp hay may ignite the whole stack.

It is the same in other spheres of life. If we are wise, we make our plans provisionally, but are prepared to modify them in detail to meet changing circumstances. Otherwise, like the farmer with his hay, we may defeat our own ends.

### *Guidance through Family and School*

Guidance at first is largely external, through family, school and friends as we grow up in a world that has a long history behind it and have to learn to take our place within it. At first the family shields the growing child while it is learning the a, b, c of life. The right laying of this foundation is one of the most important functions of the family. It mediates to the child the social values of the particular community of which it is a part. These values differ in a primitive tribe or a civilised community: but they fit the child for participation within that community. The family can only pass on the level of life by which it is actually living. This may be below or above the average level of culture, and all communities, primitive or otherwise, have some further say in the training of the child.

The school takes on the process of education, passing on the traditions and knowledge relevant to the level of tribal or national life which has been reached by the community. Then each individual is launched out into the wider world, no longer protected by family or school and no longer limited by the selective impact made upon it by parents and educators.

### *Guidance through Responsibility*

We must learn to stand on our own feet, must learn what is trustworthy and reliable in *us* and what is still imperfect, immature or distorted. Real education—a drawing out of and development of what it is in us to become—goes on from the cradle to the grave. Family and school are but our apprenticeship to life.

When we begin to take real responsibility for ourselves, God's guidance becomes more internal: though we may still not recognise it as His guidance. We learn much—both good and ill—through friends of our *own* choosing, instead of through family and school, about entering into which we had no choice. Even there, of course, we had some responsibility for making the best of what was possible, or wasting our opportunities.

As we grow up we have the responsibility for choosing the kind of work we want to do and are prepared to submit to further training to qualify for it until we can take real responsibility in it.

Then there is the most important choice of a life-partner with whom to share the privilege of founding a family ourselves.

In these ways God is guiding us to fulfil His purposes for humanity. He is leading us to become the kind of responsible people needed to carry out His plans for this small section of His universe.

But things don't always go smoothly. We find we need more than the guidance of parents, teachers, and the various authorities at work in the State and the Church. These do not all agree. We need some inner convictions to help us to steer a straight course in spite of cross-currents and difficulties. As we take our responsibilities seriously, be they little or big, we find the need to consolidate our contact with the God who causes the whole pattern, where unaided we often see only ragged edges.

### *Guidance through Desire*

Our desires make us sensitive to much that either hinders or helps their fulfilment. There may, for example, be signposts "Blackpool" so many miles: but without the desire to go to Blackpool we shall not be guided by the signs, and may even pass them without seeing them at all. We notice what is relevant to our interest and pass by much that may be of interest and value to our neighbour.

Each of us in this way sees a different cross-section of the world. Our actions are effective in proportion to our ability to recognise what is relevant and what is irrelevant to their performance. Our desires act as a focus for attention. If desires are incompatible with each other, conflict between them may be acute. We all know the strain real indecision involves. "How happy I could be with either, were t'other dear charmer away" describes one such conflict of desires in the young man who cannot marry both and yet hesitates to take the plunge with either. Yet the desire to settle down and marry is a fundamental one, so that a choice has to be made. But the very conflict may quicken his insight into the real nature of each until he can make a choice more in keeping with realities than the first fluctuating attractions of each. He has to get to know them better to decide between them and then bend all his energies to winning the one with whom he wishes to "make a real go" of marriage and its responsibilities.

So, if our desire is to find the way of God for us, and not just get our own way temporarily and then find ourselves in trouble with our neighbours, this desire will make us sensitive to much that the self-seeking and self-willed fail to perceive. Yet such guidance and reinforcement through prayer is genuinely available to those who are beginning to grow up spiritually.

We can seek to discover the laws of harmony, to discern the Mind of God, to discover how things work in God's way—which fulfils their real nature. So we gradually discover how to live more "abundantly" than the self-seeking and self-satisfied ever do. But this insight only comes in proportion to the sincerity of our desire to do whatever actually is best in the circumstances. Sometimes this involves the suffering needed to transform the consequences of the "sins, negligences and ignorances" of mankind. Sometimes it involves the zest and joy of overcoming difficulties. It brings with it the joy of creative insight and the joy of understanding love.

Ways in which we can check up on the kind of desires that are true to our deepest nature and capacities, through which such a fulfilment can come, are given in the next chapter. But it is important to realise that the nature of our desires sensitises us to differing aspects of our environment and exerts a selective influence on the life we live.

VII

# FURTHER GLIMPSES OF HOW GOD GUIDES

### *Guidance through Prayer*

IT IS IMPOSSIBLE TO PROVE TO ANYONE WITHOUT SUCH experience that prayer can help: and equally impossible to disprove it to one who has found in experience that something, or someone, *over and above his own efforts* has participated in the total result. We can feel guidance as a prompting to right action, when, with our whole being, we really want to discover and do the right, but are not sure what is right in some particular set of circumstances. How we can see this will be shown in more detail in the next chapter. We can feel the guidance of a Greater and More Comprehensive Mind in the dovetailing of many external circumstances which at first may seem to be coincidences. Later we find they are more than that. These vary with our own faithfulness to such light as we have until we dimly realise a Greater Intelligence than our own is at work behind the scenes. This seems to be in touch not only with our own minds, but with others with whom we are brought into touch at just the right time.

Dr. Christopher Woodard, in *A Doctor's Faith Holds Fast*, looks to such "signs" as indicating or confirming that he has *picked up his own cue aright* and is doing what God wants him to do at the time. He gives many examples which show this.

*Guidance through Intuition*

But there is need for warning here. It is truc that on a certain level of spiritual insight we can expect guidance through the co-operation of many, each with some tiny part to play in the whole episode, which will enable our part to fit in with an over-all pattern we can only discover as we go. But it is possible to misinterpret signs coming from levels of as yet unregulated desires, as if they were Divine. We have to use all our capacities, as Dr. Woodard stresses, and accept all human responsibility before we can count on God adding the *intuitive knowing* that links us within a wider spiritual fellowship, *seen and unseen*, than our unaided human faculties can do. Dr. Woodard said, "In spite of having had a quite considerable degree of experience and education, I try frequently to let this intuitive faculty show itself in my personal life, and as a result have been able to develop it quite considerably."

Mrs. Alice Bailey, in *From Intellect to Intuition*, also shows the wider range of intuition, but she too stresses the need for the fullest use of intellect and intelligence as well. It is the disciplined mind, she says, which can best learn how to open up the mind in meditation, and develop intuitive awareness of spiritual realities which go beyond the range of the discursive intellect. It is to a disciplined *life* Christ calls us, and through disciplined minds He can work reliably. The undisciplined may catch glimpses and find occasional healing follows their prayer or touch. It is, however, sporadic and unreliable. This is not because God is unreliable, but because they made such an intimation of a farther reach of reality a substitute for the effort of living responsibly in every area of their own lives. The attempt to specialise in healing others without seeing through their own inadequacies, or blind spots, may mean that God cannot continue to use them. As Christ said, "Many are called, but few are chosen." There are too many examples of "misguidance" which have been taken to be of

God for any facile reliance on direct guidance. We can, however, train ourselves and be willing to be trained to recognise increasingly the real inspiration and word of God. One way is:

### *Guidance through Soul's Sincere Desires*

Professor Glenn Clark, in his well-known book *I Will Lift Up Mine Eyes*,[1] stresses the need to sift and test our *desires* if our prayers are to become effective. Many prayers are attempts to coerce or cajole God into fulfilling our will, our wishes, instead of to discover and co-operate with His. Yet it is also true, as we have seen, that unless we desire something, we shall not take any steps to achieve our desire ourselves, but will be blind to any guidance or indications as to how to satisfy it.

It is here Dr. Clark is so helpful and I would like to describe a real step forward that we can *all* take at *any* time. If we follow his advice this will go a long way towards clearing out of the way misguidance from unrecognised desires in us which may have wrapped themselves up in a respectable cloak, and may even take in others as well as ourselves.

Dr. Clark advises us to take a week to try to discover "our soul's sincere desires". We are to write them out, clearly and carefully, and then go through them by the light of seven texts, one each day, amending and altering the list as this may make it necessary to do so, until we can be sure each desire rings true to our nature and is a true soul's sincere desire for which we have a right to pray with confidence. His sieve for sifting undesirable desires is St. Paul's "Finally brethren, whatsoever things are *true*, whatsoever things are *honest*, whatsoever things are *just*, whatsoever things are *pure*, whatsoever things are *lovely*, whatsoever things are of *good report*; if there be any virtue, and if there be any *praise*, think on these things".

Desires that can stand these tests, and which seem true to

[1] *I Will Lift Up Mine Eyes*, published by Arthur James, Evesham.

our nature, our opportunities and our capacities Glenn Clark calls "Soul's Sincere Desires". He also adds that the final list of desires at the end of the week, undertaken prayerfully and with sincerity in order to discover our *real* desires and not what we think we *ought* to want, will often differ considerably from the first outline. But anything that can rank as a "soul's sincere desire" Glenn Clark shows is one of the most reliable ways in which God does guide us so as to fulfil ourselves and His purpose for us within His long-term scale and plans, as it arises out of our true nature and *not out of our neurotic or sinful distortions of it*.

It is a testing experience to see which of our desires will stand up to such a scrutiny: but it is a very well worthwhile one for getting rid of many enemies within us which had been sapping the vitality needed for creative living. To any who are approaching some cross-roads in life, with some big decision to make, which will set the stage for their life in one sphere or place, it is important to clear the decks in this way before making the decision.

None of us can foresee *all* the consequences of our decisions. We are bound up within a network of domestic, social and international relationships, the contingencies of which may prevent the fulfilment of our hopes. How often someone says, "If only I'd known that before I should have acted differently."

But we can find ourselves increasingly guided into opportunities that seem "made for us" if we first sift or test our desires. This involves eliminating the more superficial and even incompatible ones, and then concentrating our energies on fulfilling our genuine long-term aims, taking advantage of every opportunity that comes our way.

The desire to be a doctor, for example, entails years of hard study and the realisation that, even when qualified, the life will be exacting and responsible. But if it is a real deep-rooted desire to help and heal, then it is one that God can bless abundantly. Dr. Woodard, himself a medical doctor, mentions a friend of his with a similar gift of healing who is training to be a doctor so as to have the fullest opportunity as possible for the exercise of his gift. Both these men find themselves "led" to those they can help with their specialised gifts, and feel that God has called them through such gifts to dedicate them and their lives to Him.

### *Guidance through Duty*

This principle, however, applies not only to those with some outstanding gifts or opportunities for training. God needs all kinds of workers to carry on the fabric of life. The humblest life is as necessary in its true functioning and range of responsibility as those who find themselves in the limelight.

I wonder if we ever stop to think of the real miracle of co-ordination and co-operation involved in being able to put a simple threepenny stamp and an address on a letter which, *within twenty-four hours*, will have been sorted out from millions of others and delivered to any part of the United Kingdom. While for a sixpenny stamp by air it will be delivered within a few days to almost any part of the civilised world.

When we think of what those letters may mean, do we ever pause to consider the thousands of sorters working all night on the trains to get them one stage nearer their destination; and the thousands of postmen who deliver them at every door, in town or country. They may bring news, good or bad. They take cheques or money orders to bring goods to our door, or help to someone in need. They may bring hope and encouragement to the sick or lonely. They allow an interchange of views which strengthen and deepen friendship. Sometimes a life may depend on a particular letter getting through to time as surely as on a surgeon's skill; delay through a mistake in sorting can be disastrous.

Every worthwhile job can be dedicated to God and the worker can find fulfilment in a "job well done".

### *Guidance through Fellowship at Work*

Moreover, all work entails working with others, and everyone can make it easier or harder for those around to get on with their part of the job in hand. Most of us at times feel the need for some guidance and help in this sphere. We are all at such different stages of development, and the habits of some irritate others. Yet even through this God can guide us, helping us to understand each other better than we could do if only thrown into congenial company with those like-minded with ourselves, who might only encourage our weaknesses. He does not want us to be alike. The varied work in the world needs people with different tastes and aptitudes. But God does want each of us to make the best of our own particular aptitudes, and not only find fulfilment in so doing, but the capacity to respect workers with different skills in a way that only the skilled themselves can appreciate adequately.

When lecturing to the troops, as I did during the war, I used to stress the fact that any major achievement depended on the success and co-ordination of thousands of efforts, none of which alone could have brought success, but that the omission of any *one* of these at a critical point could endanger the whole, so that every man's contribution counted. One example from civil life was the apparently humdrum job of the man who tapped the wheels on express trains while they were standing in a station to hear if any flaw had developed. Yet if he missed one the train might go off the rails and hundreds of lives be lost. That example came to my mind because of a train accident in which a wheel rolled off and was found some distance away. Someone had missed spotting a loose bolt at the last test.

So from another angle we see suffering may be caused through the carelessness of others. Yet awareness of this can spur us on to play our small part, whatever it may be, as reliably as possible.

### *Guidance through Reason and Faith*

Reason and faith are often superficially supposed to be in opposition. Yet they are very closely connected and there is no true faith that is not compatible with reason. This is shown clearly in St. John's Gospel.

"In the beginning was the Word [Logos, Reason, Divine Wisdom] and the Word was with God and the Word was God. The same was in the beginning with God.

"All things were made by him: and without him was not anything made that hath been made. In him was life: and the life was the light of men. And the light shineth in the darkness; and the darkness apprehendeth it not . . .

"This was the true light, even the light which lighteth every man coming into the world . . .

"As many as received him, to them gave he the right to become the children of God, even to them that believe on his name.

"Which were born, not of blood, nor of the will of the flesh, nor of the will of man, but of God.

"And the Word became flesh: and dwelt among us [and we beheld his glory, glory as of the only begotten from the Father] full of grace and truth."[1]

Here the light of reason, of the Logos, the Divine Wisdom, is a light that not only illumines all men, but through that illumination enables them to believe in Christ and discover in Him the Word made flesh, the incarnation of God. From this faith fresh powers proceed. Reason and faith are not identical, though neither can exist without the other.

We have to know Christ before we can trust Him. We have to love God with our *minds* as well as our *hearts* if we are to serve Him with the *strength* that flows through us when head and heart are in harmony and not in opposition. God guides us through honest thinking as well as loyalty and genuine devotion.

[1] St. John 1, vv. 1–5, 9, 12, 13, 14.

Faith in the possibility of ultimate harmony amidst the warring elements within the individual, and the repercussions of this in the widespread conflicts in the world, tends to find a way of working towards the goal. Disbelief closes the door to endeavour.

Faith for St. Paul was a great dynamic: faith in the power of a triumphant Saviour, faith in the power of good, of love, to overcome all evil: and according to his faith so it was unto him. Even his imprisonment in Rome, he said, was a furtherance to the Gospel, as he found all things worked together for good to those who loved God (that is, were in right relationship to reality).

This faith is not a contradiction of reason, but a fulfilment of it. The insight that made it possible sprang from a vital communion with the living Saviour who could make His presence felt after death.

The difficulties that make one give up, spur another on to greater endeavour. There are unsuspected reserves in most of us if we can only find the way to tap them. It is getting into touch with them that is the real problem.

Richard Whitwell wrote, "Therefore sincerity leads us on to the greater Truth, when its own deeper perception awakens. Without sincerity there can be no real progress at all, nor can there be that surrender which is man's yielding to God when Love Divine gives Itself to him. At this point there is a spiritual recognition or interior knowing that One has passed this way before, and planted the Standard of the Kingdom of Heaven on this earth of ours, for us to rally there. It demands our self-surrender where that standard is, and it happens to be just where we are.

"It is set in the midst of *our* earth, central to our unit life, our communal life, our national life, and the greater life of humanity, as it is central in the great Cosmos."[1]

This is finely said. When we see the Word, Logos, Reason,

[1] *In the Desert a Highway*, p. 58.

at the heart or centre of all that is, our world, ourselves, and all other created beings, we know that in spite of detours or deviations, in spite of our sins, negligences and ignorances, Divine Wisdom is able to draw us back to our true centre in it. In that faith we can find courage to overcome the whirlpools of suffering thrown up on the surface of life, secure in the deep still waters that carry us forward so silently that we do not always realise their presence beneath the froth and bubble. H. T. Hamblin often speaks of trusting the "current that knows the way".

The true guidance of spirit comes through from this deeper source ever more fully as we learn to recognise it and to trust it. Faith is not just belief. Many mistaken beliefs have been firmly and sincerely held (e.g. that the world was flat, though now we can sail or fly right round it). Faith is in a very real sense the "substance", the inner reality of being, which underlies our hope and in due course fulfils it. Faith is a quality of *life*. It is the fruit of the Spirit. What from the standpoint of the ego may seem to be mountains of difficulty, dwindle into mole hills before the spiritual resources available through faith in the ultimate Wisdom and Love of God.

### *Guidance Through the Bible*

This has been a source of guidance and inspiration to millions for nearly two thousand years, and long before that the ancient Hebrews used writings, that are included to-day in the Old Testament, as revealing the will of God and pointing the way to the Messiah, the Deliverer.

Our ideas of inspiration have changed with the centuries, and we no longer think of God as dictating every word in the Bible, which made it so difficult to understand contradictory statements. Yet all the modern research which has thrown light on this, has enabled us to see far more clearly how to recognise the Word of God in the Bible. As St. John said, "The Word became flesh and dwelt among us." The Revelation of God is through *persons.* The Bible is a collection of books written by many people at different times to illustrate or describe different aspects of God's ways to men, and it shows a steady progress from primitive ideas of a vindictive God, to the compassion of a Hosea, an Isaiah, and the supreme expression of this in Christ.

As the late Archbishop William Temple said, "What we find in the Old Testament scriptures is not mainly, if at all, authoritative declarations of theological doctrine, but living apprehension of a living process wherein *those whose minds are enlightened by divine communion can discern in part the purposive activity of God.*"[1] He goes on, "He guides the process; He guides the minds of men; the interaction of the process and the minds which are alike guided by Him is the essence of revelation."[2] Dr. Temple also stressed that the words are not the revelation, but the vehicle of it. As he said, "The precise oracles of Isaiah and Jeremiah, for example, are not in themselves revelation for others. But countless persons have been convinced that through those oracles the Word of God has come home to their own souls. And when it comes it always comes with authority, claiming obedience. What is revealed is not truth concerning God, but God Himself."[3]

The record of the life of Christ in the Gospels comes through the minds of those who knew Him and passed on what they knew of Him to others. Christ *lived* the life that has challenged man throughout the ages. But He did not dictate the record mechanically so that there would be no doubt or confusion as to what He had said and done. He used the memories of faithful but not infallible disciples, and left us to discern the true lineaments of the Divinity both *expressed in* and *concealed by* that life in spite of discrepancies and doubts as to the authenticity of some sayings or actions attributed to Him.

[1] Italics mine.
[2] *Nature, Man and God,* p. 312.
[3] Ibid., p. 354.

In doing this He was throwing upon us all the necessity for using our own insight and intuition, and so making it possible for us to respond to Him as a Person and not to a mechanically infallible record of His life.

When we realise this we can, and do, find Him speaking to us, speaking to our condition, through the pages of the Gospel, in ways that come alive as we ponder and meditate upon them. He does not usually tell us what to do in so many words, though this does seem to happen sometimes. He enables us to see what to do or how to do it through quickening the spirit within us so that we respond to a wider spiritual environment than is open to us when we are selfish, self-seeking, or self-concerned.

In *Everyman's Mission*[1] Dr. Rebecca Beard says, "There is a spiritual perception which is given to those who abide in the words of Jesus Christ and who live daily with Him. There is a kind of spiritual psychism which Jesus and the disciples knew and used and which many of the saints and mystics have known. It operates above the psychic plane and comes through the Holy Spirit. It is the Divine Wisdom leading and guiding us, telling us what we need to know. We do not voluntarily seek for it, for we know it will be given when it is needed for ourselves or for another."

In the next chapter we shall see some ways in which we may increasingly learn to discern *for ourselves* the way in which God makes Himself felt within the depths of our own mind, so quickening our spirit and perception and stimulating our obedience.

[1] P. 143. Publishers: Arthur James, Evesham.

## VIII

# MEDITATIONS ON HOW TO KNOW THE WILL OF GOD

### *How to* See *the Will of God*

LAST NIGHT A DEEP LEVEL WAS REACHED IN PRAYER, GUIDED BY an intuitive "knowing how" for a first experience of this kind. I was in a deep impasse at the time, through which I could not see how to reconcile two conflicting loyalties. I had been going through Professor Glenn Clark's *I Will Lift up Mine Eyes*, and the phrase "I will to will the will of God" came into my mind, and I found myself saying "I will to *see* the will of God", with no idea of how to "see" it. But the phrase held true, mobilising all that was in me in a deep silence to let the deeper levels of being throw up any light available. There was a quiet expectancy, and then suddenly at the cross-roads ahead was the Cross of Christ. There *was* the will of God, and it was *seen*, a visible symbol.

Deep bowed my head in awe that again a sign had come. The deeper levels *were* open and the way lay straight ahead, turning neither to the right nor to the left, through that triumphant expression of the Will of God shining through the worst anything in space and time could inflict, drawing all men to Christ. So it seemed as if He would appear on the life-road of every man, each approaching from his own direction, and finding his way to the fullness of life through that one door into the Kingdom of God that is never shut. There was no indication of what this would involve: but a very deep gratitude and feeling that I should be guided through from this deeper level until the way of God opened up and the one that could not serve Him was blocked and left behind.

This lifted me high above all anxiety for the outcome. When the Cross of Christ was planted at the cross-roads the right road would be found.

This morning I realised that I must not pray for what I wanted, but for the best that was practicable in such a way as to make it possible for God to bring the solution into sight *between* us, since others too were involved.

This was felt to be a really mature form of prayer. Not letting my own strong desire for what I wanted try to "draw it" to me —as can be done—but a more selfless prayer that was felt in some very real way made it possible for God to bring something to pass that without it He could not have done. As this high level was reached, above the conflict and confusion of my own desires was the "willed gap" that could let the truly creative forces of Spirit come into play. The issue had to be relinquished completely for some unexpected way out of the impasse to come into sight.

I did realise very deeply last night that if one's own channel *is* clear God can so work through it as to over-rule *any* external influence; though not of course to avoid its more superficial consequences. Christ's crucifixion was a real one through which He had to be true to the way of the Father for Him, under the actual circumstances and cross loyalties and fears of all concerned. But *no one* can block our real contact with God. Only we ourselves can do that. However much we can help or hinder each other—and we can do both—there is a fundamental level in each that *none* can touch save God. To bring that into focus is to release a deeper quality of life and faith than any other personal relationship makes possible. This, however, can transform all relationships by bringing the hidden Self nearer the surface.

### *How to* Hear *the Will of God*

Having found the attempt to *see* the will of God had brought first interior illumination as to *how* to see it, and then illumined a way out of the impasse that had seemed insoluble, I found myself saying, "I will to *hear* the will of God", though not knowing how to *hear* it, as I had not known how to *see* it, and yet had found the visual image of the Cross at the cross-roads was thrown up from a deeper level of being in response to my search.

For some time there was a blank, and then the phrase "The still small voice of calm" was borne in upon me as *hearing* the will of God. To hear God speak through the calm at the centre of the storm is a real hearing. The calm *is* the voice of God as the will of man and the will of God are truly aligned, and the peace of God that goes beyond understanding is experienced in a creative Silence that goes beyond all words.

Thus there is a true seeing and a true hearing of the will of God that cannot be formulated discursively. An inner way is unfolding itself as I go.

This was followed by the thought of supersonic flight, faster than sound, and also the problem of "weightlessness" involved in stratosphere flying. Though it was possible to *hear* the still small voice of calm, there was a level above or beyond hearing, beyond the range of sound and a comparable weightlessness. A freedom from earth-bound anxieties would express a true stratosphere prayer, a lightness of Spirit which increases the range and rate of activity free from the frustrations and frictions on lower levels.

### *How to* Feel *the Will of God*

Yet a further experiment followed as I tried to "will to feel the will of God" in this attempt to learn how to distinguish and discern the real impact of Spirit from the thoughts or desires arising from the subconscious. How to *feel* the will of God I did not know. But it was realised to be a genuine prayer, opening one by one every channel through which God can make His way known to us.

For a time nothing happened. Then came a real influx of power. My hands were stretched out to the limits of extension, really stretched—rigid as a rock—and I knew how to *feel* the will of God through my hands, offering them to God to use for the healing of a friend which needed "wiring for power" and not just for "light". This seemed to be a real way of feeling the will of God, as the visual image of the Cross had focused seeing it and the still small voice of calm, hearing it. The will to see, hear and feel brought an appropriate but completely unpredictable response. The channels for communication are opening up and I shall increasingly learn to discern the way God would have me go.

This is a feeling of the will of God as distinct from *knowing* it, or seeing it.

### *How to* Know *the Will of God*

We have seen how to see, hear and feel the will of God. This led me on to praying "I will to *know* the will of God", a genuine desire to know His will.

A deep peace, a lifting above discursive thought came as I stayed my mind expectantly for the Spirit to show me how to distinguish *knowing* the will of God from seeing, hearing or feeling it.

The will of God was the will of the "Whole", not my will, but God's. How could one know that? It was too vast and great for our small minds. Then came the analogy of a man knowing a woman, not knowing about her, not making a catalogue of her graces, but knowing *her* in the immediacy of their intercourse. So there was a way of "knowing" God, not knowing about Him, but an immediacy of knowing as spirit with spirit meet, through which God could make His way, His will known intuitively, not discursively.

"Intuitive knowing", yes that was a true knowledge of the will of God. Not knowing *how* we know, but knowing *what* we know; *that* we know, as a Greater Wisdom seeps into us when we genuinely seek to know the will of God. This is a knowing from above, not from below. It is a knowing proportional to the sincerity of the desire to know the Will that might over-rule our own desires, as yet being more worth while than our own will. Christ in Gethsemane could *know* the will of God while also realising it meant the complete crucifixion of His own will as an isolated self. His plea "If it be possible let this cup pass" yet "nevertheless, not my will but Thine, be done" involved a real knowing, a real recognition of a Will beyond the limits of this temporal life, as yet involving a *greater* good than His own will could accomplish. He *had* done His best, done all He could, and the people He came to help and save were rejecting Him. His will was not enough. By accepting the consequences of his rejection and making that Greater Will His own, He *knew* in Himself the will of God for man.

That is a *true* knowing of the will of God, a knowing *in oneself* in the actual setting and circumstances of life.

This is a new insight, a deeper realisation. These meditations are amplifying the way to discern the will of God before being able in Glenn Clark's phrase to "will to *will* the Will of God". A Greater Mind is illumining my own. But how can I "will to *will* the Will of God"?

### *How to* Will *the Will of God*

Faith is belief we translate into action: to will the will of God is to set in motion all the resources of Almighty God to bring it to pass. How then can I will to will the will of God? We can only *will* something believed to be possible. We may wish for things that seem impossible, but not will them. To will the will of God He must make us realise that His objective is possible, not in terms of our finite efforts, but in relation to His resources. Faith is conviction in the presence of spiritually apprehended grounds for the conviction that issues in action.

He who will *do* the will shall know, and we know *in* the doing. Will is concerned with action, not aspiration. To will the Will of God is to will the manifestation of that will on earth, in concrete detail. God wills into being our finite wills through which to effect His purposes on earth. We can only will to will the Will of God if our wills are truly aligned with the inner reality of the creative "image of God", the Divine spark within us. There is a superficial will, self-will, and there is the deeper will of the self as a whole which *can* will to will the Will of God since it arises out of our true nature as willed by God. It thus sees the possibilities within its range truly enough to will them into actuality, so fulfilling the will of God in some particular context.

*I* will to will the Will of God does not mean willing the whole activity of God which includes the whole universe within its range. It is to will the Will of God within the limited range of possibilities open to us. It means rejecting anything that appeals to, or bolsters up, the lesser self, and focusing all our energies on bringing into effect whatever has been seen, heard, felt or known to *be* the Will of God in the actual circumstances and situations which demand action.

Before being able to will the Will of God we must have become aware of it through whatever channel this awareness has come. That was why to "will to will the Will of God" at the start of these meditations seemed impossible—a real blank. How could we will the Will of the Almighty? But to realise that that Will is expressed in and through a myriad wills is to be able to dedicate our will to fulfilling the Will of God within our particular area of responsibility. Willed action is *responsible* action and not impulsive or involuntary action.

"Are you doing this of your own free-will," I was asked when the decision took shape that led out of the impasse with which these meditations started. When I said, "Yes", I realised I was acting responsibly, believing the unexpected solution to the impasse was the Will of God in the circumstances, so that I was then *willing* the Will of God and so bringing it into action.

I am learning *how* to will the Will of God by discovering I have frequently managed to will it without thinking in terms of God at the time. His Will was *in* my will when this expressed the real self acting responsibly within the whole web or mesh of circumstance in which I was placed. The freedom of the will was thus oddly enough seen to have been manifested within the restricting and frustrating circumstances that seemed to make freedom impossible. In willing to find the best way actually possible, and refusing to let the effort go until this was achieved, one *is* willing the Will of God which becomes effective within the heart of all that seems to oppose it. Thus even the evil elements, the cross loyalties, and the mistakes which have contributed to some impasse are used by God to fulfil His will in and through them.

To will the Will of God is to will the will of the Whole, of all that is, and not just the narrowly good from our limited human range of knowledge. This makes it possible for Him to bring about what He wants in spite of clashes on our lower levels. We can only will what is possible, and to will God's solution when we can see no way out of some frustrating situation, is to believe He *can* open out a way we ourselves would never have envisaged, and yet which we find is more true to and for us than anything we could have foreseen. This will has to be maintained over whatever period is necessary for all the forces in opposition in an impasse to be harmonised from a level *above* the conflict so that *each* contributes some essential element to the solution and none is left out to "come back at us again".

The Will of God still has to be willed by *us* to win *our* freedom in His service which alone can fulfil our truest desires.

Every failure makes it harder, as every success in being true to our deeper nature increases the range within which responsibility is real and *effective* within the world of action.

To see, hear, feel or know the Will of God is *within* us: to will the Will of God is to externalise that and brings it into being in the world of common purposes in which we all share. We know in the doing, as the skill of a tennis player lies in his actions: not in his knowledge about them or about the rules of the game. St. James said, "I will show you my faith *by* my works".

To will the Will of God *now* is to accept the past as it has been to be taken up constructively, just as it is, with all its blots and failures, its "triumphs and disasters", as the matrix which sets the stage for the next phase. It is to will the resultant of the Whole, and not what might have seemed more desirable if particular mistakes had not been made. The potentialities for the future are conditional upon, though not caused by, the assimilation of the past. The more complete the assimilation is, the greater is the range of freedom and opportunity for the future, as by the Grace of God we transmute the past into a creative future through which the Eternal and Timeless transcends its temporal manifestations within the Whole that includes all.

The recognition of the central importance of a Spirit which is timelessly operative *within* the temporal changes and chances of life, leads on naturally to the part played by Spirit in health and healing. This forms the substance of the next chapter.

IX

# THE SPIRITUAL FACTOR IN HEALING

"A CUP OF COLD WATER MAY SAVE A LIFE, A PINT OF BLOOD given for transfusion may save another, an injection of penicillin may save a third, and the love and faith of someone who has learned through prayer how to provide a link between a sufferer and the 'life more abundant' that in their sickness they cannot respond to or appropriate unaided, may save others."

This quotation from the preface to my book, *New Concepts of Healing*, is taken from the dust-cover, as selected by the publishers.[1] In this chapter our chief concern will be with the contribution that can be made to mental, physical or spiritual health through prayer, through love and faith and through a deeper understanding of the spiritual factor in health itself. This is not to deprecate the importance of medical work: but it is to explore the neglected field of spiritual therapy, towards which psychosomatic medicine and psychiatry are reaching out.

One reviewer of my book says, "Like myself she gives her whole-hearted blessing to those with the gift of spiritual healing, emphasises the therapeutic value of prayer, but reminds us that real healing involves 'a transformation of life and not just an attempt to call down some magical power to heal without attempting to remove the causes of the disease that arises from our human failure to put first things first'."

The emphasis in my present book on suffering as a consequence of "sins, negligences and ignorances" carries the

[1] Hodder & Stoughton, England, and The Association Press, New York.

idea further. It shows in more detail how much can be done to relieve suffering by getting back to the spiritual roots of our lives and the necessity for response to a wider spiritual environment than the "natural" man can reach by his own efforts. Our participation in this wide spiritual fellowship which includes members of all ages, races and periods of history is recognised as due to Grace. It is a quality of spiritual life that is given. It is imparted from a higher dimension of Being, and therefore not limited to our finite understanding—or misunderstanding—of the laws appropriate to membership within it. Christ called it the Kingdom of Heaven, likening it to a pearl of great price that was worth a man's selling all he possessed to buy it.

Perhaps one might think of it like this. Sometimes foreigners who have lived in Britain find our way of life, our laws, our customs, more desirable and satisfying than in their own land. So they apply for a transfer, apply to be "naturalised Britishers", subject to and profiting by the laws of the land of their adoption.

So we may seek to become "naturalised citizens of the Kingdom of Heaven", obeying its laws and gaining the privileges of a wider fellowship than our natural citizenship, whether that be British, American, Russian, Chinese, or any other of the many distinctive nationalities in the world.

In "What think ye of Christ?" I have tried to show that the coming of Christ inaugurated a fresh stage in evolution. Just as the appearance of life, mind and spirit successively transcended the modes of functioning of the previous levels, revealing fresh and hitherto unsuspected capacities, so the kingdom Christ came to establish on earth brought a whole range of fresh capacities, fresh potentialities within our reach. This idea throws a lot of light on the phenomena of spiritual healing, as well as on many other contemporary problems.

The permeation of the new "aeon", or age, by the spirit of Christ can be seen to be a long-term policy, and a measure of conflict with even the best that preceded it can be expected until the whole of life is "baptised into Christ". He himself could say that none greater than John the Baptist had been born of woman, yet that He who was little in the Kingdom of Heaven was greater than he. (Cf. A child to-day being able to flood a room with light with a turn of a switch, when the wisest men in the pre-scientific ages could not even see the possibility of such a "miracle").

Each stage in evolution widens the range of environment within which and to which response is possible. The coming of Christ opened up another dimension of reality to us, a fresh kingdom with its own laws capable of combining the laws of behaviour in the lower kingdoms creatively as each of these in turn had done previously in connection with the kingdom next below it. It is the nature of these laws we need to discover and apply in our own lives, and those of others, for a true recovery of "Spiritual healing".

If a crystal could talk it would say to a cell or a plant, "What you are doing is impossible. Things don't grow like that in my world. You must be a dream, not a reality." If a plant could talk to an animal it would say, "What you are doing is impossible. Life must stay put where it is. You can't walk about like that. You're just imaginary." If animals could talk to men they would say, "You can't alter things by thinking about them. You're got to take what comes. You can't see ahead. Thinking only goes on in the imagination, not in reality." Yet man builds his cities, his rail-roads, his ships and his planes because he can use conceptual thinking to make better use of all that "comes to him" perceptually through his senses.

So when "natural man" and Christian man meet, natural man says, "You can't do that, nature doesn't work like that. Force counts, and when nature has run down there's nothing left. Spirit is only a pipe-dream, not a reality."[1]

[1] Natural man and Christian man may not always be two separate individuals. The conflict between the old and the new occurs in each of us as soon as we have caught a real glimpse of the reality of the new way of life in Christ and find the pull back of the old is in us as well.

But Christian man says, "No. When you come to the end of natural resources you find a new *kind* of energy, a new *dunamis* or dynamic can take over. By relinquishing effort, by seeing the whole from a different angle, by seeing time within the setting of eternity, so many fresh activities become possible that it is like being born again, born into a wider world into which Christ has opened the door for man."

This is the sphere within which true spiritual healing is operative. Within this kingdom by fresh combinations of the laws of nature results can be achieved that go beyond them. Only a century ago it would have been thought impossible to make planes, so much heavier than air, carry the tremendous loads they do to-day. Yet that miracle, counteracting the force of gravity, has not broken nature's laws. Intelligence has mastered them sufficiently to combine them to rise above gravity. Intelligence, however, is a spiritual capacity, not a mechanical one. Its application involves insight into the nature of the laws of behaviour or being through which fresh combinations can extend the range of *action* in the external world. As we have seen, God guides us through intelligent insight and not by shouting instructions we could not understand.

So when we come to healing, to lifting the great burden of disease, we must make use of all the knowledge gained on every level of life. We must recognise the regenerative healing power in nature that at once sets to work to repair injuries.

We must recognise the amazingly intricate balance that life is maintaining in us all the time, and must foster the conditions that give this vis medicatrix naturae a chance to carry out its healing work. After a bone has been fractured, for example, doctors can set the bones into the correct position and fix the limb with splints or plaster. Then nature will set to work to grow fresh bone tissue to re-join the fractured ends. If the bone has been badly set, nature will still make a join, but with a crooked limb it may not stand the strain of use.

But as we have seen, much disease is either caused by or

complicated by emotional factors. Mental or moral conflicts the personality has not been able to solve satisfactorily need psychological or spiritual treatment to focus them clearly. Like bringing the broken ends of bone together, this gives the mind as a whole a chance to assimilate the experience that had been disruptive. There is a natural healing power in the psyche as well as in the body which we can rely on if we "know how".

One bit of practical advice I used to give when lecturing on how to stand up to war strain was that if some particular scene of horror stuck in one's mind the thing to do was to associate it with some particular element within it for which one could be thankful—e.g. in some of the worst mutilations "well, at least they couldn't have felt anything, that would have killed them outright". As soon as something the mind *can* accept with thankfulness is associated in this way with *any* distressing experience, it is open to the healing effect of the rest of our mind, which holds a lot of pleasant memories as well as painful ones.

On another level we have seen that bitterness can be changed to forgiveness and so open the way to a renewed relationship, when we realise the value of the relationship that made us vulnerable. There is a level of redemptive love that can transcend broken relationships on the natural level, raising them up into the Kingdom of Heaven.

This brings us within the specifically spiritual realm. This is true whether the transformations of negative soul-destroying emotions into positive outgoing relationships to others occur in a psychiatrist's consulting room, a pastor's study, the confessional or even the room of a friend. In some cases such re-adjustments lead to the disappearance of physical symptoms of illness. In others something more is needed, either medically, psychologically, psychically or spiritually before the outworking of diseased processes can be overcome.

Amongst these the effects of prayer and the work of healers who rely on prayer, touch or sacrament must be considered.

Examples are occurring to-day in too many parts of the world and in many different denominations to be mere chance. It is not always realised that the development of Christian Science, Spiritualism, Psychical Research, Parapsychology, the Oxford Groups, innumerable faith healing movements, Truth Centres, Medical Psychology and the revival of the Churches' Ministry of Healing, have all arisen within the last 100 years. It is natural, therefore, that there should be some confusion in this field, with so many rival theories, all of which are producing *some* results that just cannot be ignored.

### *World-Wide Movements of the Spirit*

A few centuries before Christ there seemed to be a similarly world-wide movement of spirit from the eighth to the fourth century B.C. It took different forms in different races and communities. The influence of the Hebrew prophets on the one hand; the influence of Buddha in North India, and that of Confucius in China, have left their mark on all subsequent development. Within the same period Socrates, Plato and Aristotle in Greece began the emancipation of the human mind in other directions. About the same time that Hippocrates was laying the foundation for medical science by accurate observation of symptoms, simultaneously Roman genius developed the idea of law and justice as binding upon man. Our whole Western culture is based on the Hebrew, Greek and Roman contributions to *permanently valid elements in human experience.*

Yet this has been inadequate to avoid two recent world wars. There is an increasing recognition that the East has something to contribute to the West, as well as the West to the East. Only as this interchange can be effected in harmony, to the benefit of both, can the foundation of World Peace be established soundly.

The Spirit again seems to be stirring on a world-wide scale. At the same time as the nations whose fundamental economy was pre-scientific are reaching out to the West for modern technical knowledge and equipment to raise the standard of living of their peoples, many thinkers in the West are reaching out for deeper spiritual insights to Eastern thinkers who had explored further into the depths—and heights—of the human psyche than we had, in order to enrich our own knowledge and experience. Amongst others Professor Alan Watts has made very real contributions. His *Legacy of Asia* and *Behold the Spirit*, are a real blend of the best in East and West. Geraldine Coster, in *Yoga and Western Psychology*, has also combined insight into East and West.

### *Healing*

Striking examples of healing long-standing physical disease are coming from many different quarters of the world, which seems to indicate a further range of healing radiations available to us that function through, or are focused by, specific individuals. Several such examples are quoted in my *New Concepts of Healing*.

Another striking example may be included from *Christ Still Healing*[1] by Elsie H. Salmon.

*Instantaneous healing of mastoid torticollis.* Miss E. C., Newquay.

"Eighteen years ago the nerves and muscles on the left side of my neck collapsed. The condition was diagnosed as 'mastoid torticollis' and as being akin to polio. I was examined through the years by many eminent doctors and specialists in England and in Europe—one being General Rommel's personal specialist in Germany—always with the same pronouncement, 'We can perhaps ease the condition, but we cannot cure you.' Treatments were advised and resorted to; often over long periods with little avail.

"I went to Torquay and received from Mrs. Salmon the laying on of hands. *Immediately* adhesions broke up and a

[1] *Christ Still Healing*. Publishers: Arthur James, Evesham. 11/- post free.

life-giving glow surged through my veins. The mastoid muscle which had been lifeless for years is now practically normal and I am able to 'pull' on it. Every day brings new and greater freedom."

Mrs. Salmon then gives a little of the background of this case. "This young woman of about thirty-eight years of age had been suffering for over eighteen years when she came to me. The head was deeply embedded in the shoulders and was immovable: the eyes were crossed and sight and balance affected. Not only had specialists in this country tried to help her but also eminent specialists on the continent, but without avail. She was desperate.

"She received the laying on of hands privately. After the treatment we were standing chatting quietly when I felt impressed to use my fingers again on the back of her neck. They were guided to manipulate rapidly on the neck and at the top of the spine; after which we heard 'crackling like the crushing of dried greaseproof paper' and the head was immediately released as adhesions were broken down. The head and neck lifted itself out of the shoulders in which it had been embedded for so many years. She was able to stand upright. It was an amazing experience for us both. She called again the following morning and by this time the eyes had straightened out."[1]

Agnes Sanford, in *The Healing Light*, writes, "Many people to-day are unwilling to recognise the operation of a spiritual power through the being (body) of man because they feel it is unscientific. No one would have believed a few years ago that an orchestra playing in London could be heard in Paris. They would have said that such a thing was unscientific. Yet it was not contrary to the laws of nature. It was only a bit in advance of man's understanding of the laws of nature. So it is with the power of God that works through the being of one person for the healing of another.

[1] *Christ Still Healing*, p. 84.

"It is not really 'unscientific' at all. It is only the channelling of a flow of energy from God's being through man's being. It is the entering in of the Holy Spirit of God through the Spirit of man; via the conscious and subconscious mind of that man, via the nerves of his body into the patient's inner control centre and thence to his mind and his spirit. The nerves are the telegraph wires of the body. The one who prays connects the nerve terminals in his hands with the nerve terminals of the patient's body and through that simple and natural thought-track sends a message to the patient's subconscious mind. This message is not sent from the level of the healer's mind nor even from the level of his spirit, but from the Spirit of God Himself who moves in a mysterious way through the spirit, the mind and the body of the healer into the body, the mind and the spirit of the patient. Thus the healer makes of his whole being, spirit, mind and body, a receiving and transmitting centre for the power of God. He offers and presents to God Himself, his soul and body, as a holy and living sacrifice, which is his reasonable service.

"God works immutably and inexorably by law," Mrs. Sanford goes on. "Until mankind learns and keeps the laws of life, God's will cannot be made fully manifest. He has never from the beginning until now healed anyone by the interposition of an arbitrary or capricious force. But He heals continually *by the addition of a higher spiritual energy to a lower physical energy*. Doctors call this 'nature' and confess that they cannot always predict what nature will do."[1]

The Rev. Jim Wilson, chaplain to the Guild of Health, writes, "The healing work of Christ was not merely His deep compassion for the troubles and sufferings of men. It was an essential part of His whole work of redemption. It was part of His Gospel. The world and human nature and human souls and bodies are all made by Him to be the means of expressing

[1] *The Healing Light* by Agnes Sanford, pp. 95–7. Publishers: Arthur James, Evesham. 10/- post free.

the wholeness (or holiness) of God. He came to clean up the mess wrought in God's world by sin, and to perfect His creation: and sickness and disease are part of the evil of the world.

"The healing ministry of the Church is therefore an essential part of its whole ministry: without it, the Gospel is not preached in its fullness, which perhaps explains part of the indifference of so many to the Church's message to-day.

"The cause of much disease is to be found in wrong assumptions about God and about life, in wrong ways of thinking, which create deep disharmony in the soul, in wrong attitudes to people and to the circumstances of life. In some cases there may be no short cut back to health and healing. The person who is sick must be taught to know God truly and to change his ways of thinking, to repent his sins."[1]

He goes on, "The Church is healing people to-day . . . The quiet work goes on. I myself have had experience of the healing of asthma, meningitis, gall stones, tuberculosis, cancer, septicaemia, detached retina, a case of broken bone, and a great many others: and there are many people having similar experience all over the world. Many doctors now recognise the fact of such healing, and welcome the co-operation of those who exercise this ministry with theirs. But it is not enough to tell people about cases of healing which we know.

"It is true that Christ still heals, but the sick must be taught to know that Christ is a reality, and that, by the fact of His Ascension, His spirit is within them and it is He who will heal them. They must be taught to become conscious of His life and spirit within."[2]

Dr. Rebecca Beard asks, "How do we picture the God to whom we pray? Do we pray to the God of the Old Testament or to the God of the New? If we pray to the God most characteristic of the Old Testament, we pray to a God of caprice and impulse, of reward and punishment. If we pray to

[1] *Healing Through the Power of Christ*, pp. 61–2.
[2] Ibid., p. 38.

the Heavenly Father of the New Testament, as Jesus Christ knew Him, we pray to a God of law and order without variableness or shadow of turning. The former is the God of superstition and blind faith; the latter is the God of science founded upon factual observation and experience. The former often tempts us to acts of participation and bargaining: the latter leads us on to the mature concept of obedience and acceptance of conditions required of us for our growth and development."[1]

In another place referring to intercession, Dr. Beard says of the healing love of Christ, "As we offer ourselves for its transmission, we can actually feel the current of life flowing through us. We are giving a transfusion of life to another."[2]

All these claim that they are used and guided from a level beyond themselves which is spiritual. Harry Edwards, a spiritualistic healer, claims that the spirits of some who had been doctors on earth do the actual work through him. The others referred to claim the power of Christ working through them.

What seems to be significant is that in all these "healers" we see consecrated personalities genuinely concerned about human suffering who have found some spontaneous experience of healing through them that opened up a realm of power the reality of which they could not doubt. They then gave up their time and strength to channel it to sufferers, as doctors, psychiatrists and nurses give their time, skill and experience to mediate healing through their channels.

Skill on all levels has to be acquired by experience. Eastern teachers say that psychic healing powers show themselves at a certain stage of training as a Yogi: but that they can be a hindrance to the full spiritual development the aspiring Yogi is seeking. If, however, he can accept the reality and then leave them behind, letting go in this way the *outward signs of his inner*

[1] *Everyman's Mission*, p. 125. Publishers: Arthur James, Evesham.
[2] Ibid., p. 135.

*growth*, a subsequent turn of the spiral of growth will bring him into touch with them again when he is mature enough not to be seduced by "results" that show from the *true inner discipline* that is essential to the right use of all acquired skills.

Professor Glenn Clark, from another angle, says a "miracle" in the outer world is a secondary consequence of a deep inner and intensely sacred spiritual experience: but by the time the outward result was reported, the majority of people thought *it* was the miracle, and missed the supreme significance of the inner spiritual attitude. Dr. Woodard, like Professor Glenn Clark, sees the outward sign as a consequence of a genuine inner commitment of the sufferer to God. Both of these seek to give the priority to God, to trust His judgement, who alone knows all the conditions.

This seems to me to be a sounder approach than that of those who seek to claim or demand that healing should follow their ministrations. It is often possible by the potency of their faith and the power of the suggestion to produce results which seem to warrant their claim to "cure"; yet which do not last, because the *central need of the personality had not been met*. The real *inner* change, essential to future spiritual growth, may even be more difficult for God to evoke than if what should be a process of growth is unduly forced. Wise and experienced healers are, of course, aware of this. But many in the first flush of discovery that power can "go through them", tend to use it as a magic panacea for all ills, and blame a patient's lack of faith, instead of their own lack of skill, when something goes wrong.

It is because I am convinced that there is a vast realm of almost untapped power to which we are just becoming receptive, that I find myself so often warning would-be enthusiasts against dabbling in something they cannot control intelligently. The need for real training is a crying one if any ministry of healing s to become at least as responsible a one as the medical services are to-day. A doctor has to work hard to qualify. He has to be able to justify whatever treatment he has given to other *qualified* men, and he is disqualified from his practice if he abuses his position of confidence.

Christian Science practitioners, of whom there are about 10,000 now, are trained and registered within their religious organisation as competent to help and heal the sick. They have a body of actual experience to go upon, and, though they use spiritual and not physical means, for their healing, they, too, can be checked by fellow practitioners, trained in the same way.

A standard of training and recognition for lay psychotherapists has long been needed to eliminate the "quacks" who take a short cut to "practise". The present confusion, with so many "healing cults" developing without any real discipline, needs careful consideration. We quite obviously, to put it crudely, can't tie the Holy Spirit up within a regulation and say, "I'm sorry, you can't come in here, you are not wearing the right label." Yet the claim to work under direct inspiration without any safeguards is a very dangerous one. The Quakers check their guidance by the Inner Light in fellowship. It arises within a community who have shared in the discipline of corporate silence as they wait on the Spirit. It is a corporate, not just an individual achievement.

Elsie H. Salmon stresses the need for learning to recognise the voice of Christ, the prompting of Christ, and to be able to distinguish it from all others. Her own training in discrimination, as I know, was long and severe. For three years after her "call" to direct healing, she was bidden to say nothing about it, and to tell those who had been healed through her not to refer it to her. This rings true to Christ's telling some He had healed to go away and say nothing.

### *Healing Missions*

The absence of any spiritual diagnosis at healing missions brings with it the risk of removing temporarily hysterical simulations of organic disease without unmasking the emotional conflict responsible for them and resolving this spiritually. This is one of the reasons why many of those who have had to deal with psychological casualties distrust healing missions. This is true even if they also recognise the reality of charismatic gifts in some particular healers and even if they know the reality of many otherwise incurable diseases being healed through prayer.

Yet I think it may also be true that some resistant and chronic conditions would be most likely to be healed at a service with many others, and not by private ministrations. Worship is a corporate act. Where many are "gathered together with one accord" there can be a greater outpouring of Spirit, and sufferers can be more easily lifted above the consciousness of their disabilities and so present less obstacle to healing in such an atmosphere than when alone.

But this means that there must be adequate preparation of the sick beforehand, by clergy, ministers or lay healers, with a recognition of the real need and the presence of a praying, believing congregation whose outgoing love and compassion provide a channel for God's healing power to reach those in need.

It is, of course, true that not all who come to healing services recover: while some ministered to privately do get better. Moreover, some with no active ministrations, either privately or at a public service, at times "perceive within themselves that they are healed" at the touch of a Presence they recognise and trust. Sometimes these can be traced to coincide with the prayers of friends or prayers on their behalf in church. But in others the initiative seems to come from the side of the unseen and the inner spiritual response to this *precedes* the outer manifestation. Many more people have such sacred experiences about which they do not speak for fear of being misjudged or unbelieved than is often realised. But they have no doubt of the reality of the Grace that changed their lives, and the rest of their lives is spent in humbly seeking to serve and follow the Presence that had set them free from some crippling disability, physical, psychological or spiritual.

### *God will not be confined within our Finite Measures*

Yet He bids us ask, seek and knock. We must try to discern the spiritual laws which enable Him to heal the diseases that cripple body, mind or spirit, so that His hand may not be stayed through our indifference, our ignorance or our exclusiveness.

While Christ healed many during His earthly life we are told explicitly that in some places He could do no mighty works because of their unbelief. Teaching and healing must go together. The realisation that something has been left out, or distorted, in the historical development of Christianity with the loss of a healing ministry is hopeful. Attempts on so many sides are being made to bring it back as a normal part of Christian life.

Spiritualism and Christian Science respectively would not have arisen independently if the "communion of saints" and the capacity to "heal the sick" respectively had not got so overlaid with superstitions that they were officially suspect and dropped out of the practice of prayer and official Christianity.

The "elders of the Church" whose prayers were efficacious in New Testament days were surely those who had graduated into the dynamic life of the Spirit and could therefore become effective channels for such healing as could be mediated through prayer.

### *Intercession*

Effective intercession is an over-flow to others of a measure of real communion with God. It is not just a wishful-thinking petition, as much so-called intercession is. It arises out of a deeper level of being that is in touch with spiritual resources that go beyond the natural, or even the psychic, capacities of man. The faith that removes mountains of disability is a faith grounded in actual experience of the unseen spiritual environment within which our lives are lived.

As we have seen real prayer is a two-way line of communication. We cannot always see or understand God's plan, either for our own lives or for those of others. In proportion, as we learn to keep "tuned in" spiritually, however, we become more sensitive to the stirrings of spirit and to the presence of power to meet some need. The Quakers often find what they call "a concern" for someone is borne in upon them as they pray. They then hold this need in the creative silence of their prayer until a conviction is felt that it has been met. We have probably all experienced this sometimes, and found later that our intuitive response has been relevant and effective.

Intercession does not mean begging God to do something for our friends that He does not want to do. It means opening a channel that He can use to meet the needs of those for whom we pray in the way He sees to be best. When someone is ill, or depressed, it is more difficult for them to realise and respond to the Presence of God. Our link with them and with God may act as a transformer, so to speak. It may step up their capacity for response, and step down the full range of a power beyond their capacity to realise. The keynote in effective intercession is fellowship, both with those for whom we pray, and with God.

When Mrs. Elsie Salmon first discovered God was using her to heal, she said, "He needs a link. He does the work, but He needs my hands." Our prayers can also provide the link or channel He needs. But no mere form of words suffices. *The need has to be taken into our own hearts if we are to raise it up to God and release His power to meet it.* That is the cost of real intercession. It is also a measure of our faith in the love and wisdom of God, which is ever seeking to save that which is lost, to heal the sick and to bind up the broken-hearted.

### *The Communion of Saints*

The communion of saints surely presupposes the reality of the links with those who have passed from the sight of our physical eyes, but not from the range of our love, or we from theirs.

Psychical research, spiritualism and parapsychology are different but complementary approaches, all of which bear witness to activities of the psyche, or soul, which are not tied so closely to time and space as sense perceptions. The real world includes more than we can perceive through our senses. Infra-red rays below the level we can see and ultra-violet rays above it, show that there is more "of a kind" with that which we do perceive than the narrow range of our eyesight shows. A very slight extension would alter the appearance of our familiar world.

Telepathy shows we can become aware of the thoughts of another mind, independently of distance, if we are *en rapport.* Clairvoyance shows objects can also be perceived independently of distance and through normally completely opaque material.

Some experiences are more easily accounted for by real communications between the living and the so-called dead than any other hypothesis: though much of what passes for them is more likely to be due to wishful thinking and the inter-action between the subconscious minds of both sitters and mediums.

If, therefore, some aspects of our minds are not tied to sense perceptions and inter-action with the material phenomena of the world, then the survival of these after death becomes probable. A continuum—a spiritual world of inter-relation-ships—within which the invisible and intangible aspects of personality may be functioning, and within which survival and recognition can persist when the body no longer makes a link with material conditions, would include the facts of psychical research, religious experience and spiritual healing within the same "world" in which we now live.

Death, on this view, would extend the range of personality by bringing into focus another dimension of the same universe. Telepathic influence might thus affect the course of events through a real "communion of saints" within a mankind which was a unity of the dead, the living and those yet unborn, without whose contribution the process cannot be completed. St. Paul could refer to those who had lived by faith without receiving the promise, saying "That apart from us they should not be made perfect".[1] If that is true, then we without those yet to come cannot be made perfect either.

This is all considered much more fully in *New Concepts of Healing* than space allows here. In it a chapter on Spiritual Healing and the New Physics brings into sight a real harmony between the scientific and religious attempts of man to find his place in so vast and bewildering and fascinating a universe, and shows the importance of every human life within it.

The evidence that is accumulating from so many sides to-day does seem to show we can not only "know something about" the great universe in which we live, as if it were purely external to us, but that in prayer we find a responsive Intelligence that answers our spoken or unspoken appeal.

One striking example of this was when I was helping a woman with a badly swollen finger with a whitlow under the nail. As I prayed some power came into it and it began to bend, though it had been too stiff for her to move it before. I felt heat radiating from it as I held it in one hand with the other on her head. Then I found myself saying spontaneously and interiorly to *whoever* was transmitting it, "More heat, please", and *more heat came*! Some other Intelligence was aware of, and capable of responding to, my *silent* request. The net

[1] Hebrews 11, v. 40.

result was that within four days the whitlow had disappeared and the skin healed under the surface of the nail, which lifted up and came away spontaneously. The doctor had previously said it might go on for several weeks unless he took the nail off, which would be painful for about ten days. As it was, the process of healing was greatly speeded up and only a nick was needed to detach the nail. The finger did not even need a bandage.

The Spirit is moving on the face of the waters and some patterns are taking shape within the chaos and confusion. But this needs a chapter to itself.

## X

## THE PATTERN IN THE COSMOS

A SNOWFLAKE UNDER A MICROSCOPE IS A THING OF REAL beauty which is hidden from sight when in the mass. So, too, the delicate tracery of Jack Frost on the window panes shows a harmony of design that would tax our greatest artists to reproduce.

Have you ever taken a walk in the country after the rain and seen myriads of cobwebs gleaming with drops of water, scintillating like diamonds, and all the flowering grasses shown up in greater detail and beauty by the raindrops on them flashing back the sunlight?

Another glimpse of hidden beauty may be unknown to some readers. A cross-section of the spine of a sea urchin is like a rose window in a cathedral, so beautifully is it designed. Moreover, even in insects or animals that outwardly seem ugly there is an amazingly intricate design within the various parts to enable them to function as a unity. The same is true of our own bodies. We rarely realise the miracle of co-ordination involved in the harmony of more brain cells in a single human brain than there are people on earth! Yet the fact that each of us can raise a hand when we want to, or decide where to go for a holiday, depends upon these millions of cells functioning in harmony under the control of *one* mind. Yet each cell has its own part to play, and we soon realise the interdependence of the various parts of our bodies when something goes wrong in any part of it. A septic finger not only gives rise to pain, but we realise how unobtrusively it had been doing its work by the clumsiness we find when it is stiff and useless. So with infections anywhere—their effect spreads through the whole system and we realise we are a unity of millions of different parts. Yet also we cannot be wholly identified with any one part. The brain cannot function without the blood. Variations in the constitution of the blood either in disease, or through drugs, can alter our perception of, and reaction to, the outer world. Truly we are marvellously and wonderfully made.

The realisation that these many million cells in our bodies can function as a unity under the control of some specific intention on our part may make it easier to realise the possibility of an over-ruling Providence that can work through the differing functions of the millions of human beings so as to bring about results that none of them individually could foresee or plan. Yet these arise through each playing his, or her, limited role in the particular bit of the scheme in which he finds himself.

So often we are intimidated by mere numbers and may think "How on earth can God keep count of, or in touch with, so many millions of minds?" Yet if we can produce effects in our own bodies and through our own actions which involve the control of *more* millions of cells than there are people in the world, then the Greater Mind that made us and the world can conceivably work out *His* purpose through us and through the interactions between human beings and our environment.

It sometimes helps to think of this like an orchestra which the Great Composer is also conducting. The harmony depends upon each playing his small part in tune and in time with the rest. Being human, however, we do not always manage to keep in tune or in time with our fellows or with the Conductor, and there is a discord, with suffering and distress as a consequence. In modern music some intervals that were heard as discords a generation ago have been woven into harmonies by composers like Schnabel, Gustav Holst, Scriabin and many others.

This may give us a clue as to the possibility that the Great Composer may weave even our discords, our sins and suffering, into an over-all design that is harmonious because the discords are blended in time with overtones that modulate them into a satisfying but more comprehensive harmony.

Every element in a great symphony is needed and every kind of instrument has to play its part, yet each only "rings true" because it comes in at the right time and place in relation to the rest and the value lies in the whole, not in any section. The total effect varies according to where sections in a minor key occur. The note of triumph in a grand finale is far more inspiring when it follows a lament, an expression of the poignant element in human experience that goes too deep for words. Yet the lament, the poignancy that alone would be unbearable, can stir us to the depths and purify some of our pettier emotions precisely because it is part of a whole which by wringing victory out of defeat itself contributes to the actual structure of the ultimate triumph. Bach's Passion Music is perhaps one of the finest examples of a beauty expressed in and through and triumphing over agony and anguish.

Within the symphony that is taking form, we can either increase the harmonies or the discords, so that each can contribute some tiny fraction of the beauty of the whole. Where discords come in, the Great Composer's capacity to weave them into a higher harmony through overtones that blend is no painless wave of His wand. Discords can only be transcended when love reaches down into the very arena of suffering and by sharing in it voluntarily brings out the overtones that can enable the music to go on as *music*, not mere *noise*. Moreover, music has an invisible structure, a pattern of possible melodies and harmonies of its own, and so has our life.

Discords go on where individual players insist on bringing *their* notes in when *they* wish, instead of in time and in tune with others. If we realise that such discords are an agony to the sensitive Composer who is striving to bring harmony out of the whole, we become more sensitive ourselves to the need to "tune in". So the very pain caused by disharmony is an element in the overtones that alone can bring it within a wider harmony than we poor players, of ourselves, could ever envisage.

The musical analogy of patterns which can modify the harmony of sequences of notes in different keys can give us another glimpse into the hidden "patterns" within us which may modify our conscious aims and actual behaviour. The composer of a symphony bears in mind the actual possibility of the various keys and instruments and then, though he wants the best from his players, he does not expect the impossible.

So in life, if we look at it on the large scale, always some are suffering, sinning, dying, while others are rejoicing, growing strong and healthy and finding life worth living. The total picture is not one of gloom, whatever our newspapers may show. Two *facts* can dispel pessimism. One is that the sex instinct in man, unlike that in animals, is not seasonal but persists all the year round. Though lots of troubles arise from that, its real purpose is to forge a permanent link between man and woman while they bring up a family and not just an intermittent affair for the bringing of a child into being. In that link in which *affection and responsibility are combined* we have a real expression of the primacy of love over force or human beings could not have survived at all. Though some families are unhappy, the majority must succeed or the race would diminish.

The second fact is closely related to this. The birth of every human baby is an expression of God's trust in the claims of the weak and defenceless as being ultimately stronger than force or aggression. The long period in which a child is *completely* dependent on some adult, and will die without that care, draws out the best in mankind. The fact that the race is increasing in spite of war and disease shows more love and care *is* being expended than destruction—though the latter is still widespread enough to be a challenge to us to try to eliminate it to give *all* children the chance of a full life.

From our side, the more we learn about the hidden patterns, the rules of living laid down in and through the history of the race, the better we are able to read the score and adjust our conscious behaviour to actual capacities. We have all got to learn how to play our own specific instruments, with our differing talents and counterbalancing limitations, as well as how to blend with others.

We can also learn how to keep in tune and in step if we can discern something of the general over-all pattern within which all the smaller harmonies and discords of life find their place. Everyone has *some* philosophy of life, and the nearer this is to the underlying truth and reality of it, the more effective their lives become. Intelligent anticipation and the setting of a mood to variations in tempo and key help us to pick up our cue and tune in at the right moment.

Moreover, we can also improve our playing through some sympathy with the Conductor. Differences between merely good conductors and the genius do not only lie in technical skill and knowledge, but in a capacity to establish an emotional rapport between the orchestra members themselves and the conductor.

So if we wish to "tune in" with the Creative Mind so as to anticipate His "timing" by that fraction of a second that secures correct performance, we find thousands before us have found in prayer a way of becoming responsive to His prompting and growing out of the clash of discords into greater harmony.

This again begins to reveal the elements of "pattern" in the Cosmos. Men and women in all ages, and from all races, are strangely unanimous in some of the essentials of the process wherein our lesser minds can become attuned to the Greater Mind who made them. They have charted rocks, reefs, cul-de-sacs, and won through to the open road that lies ahead of *every* man willing to seek it and ready to follow it.

The pattern shows not only *within* the personal life as an

orderly controlling intelligence harmonises more primitive instincts, but interpersonally and within the world of action.

This shows on two levels. We are realising through telepathy, clairvoyance and pre-cognition, as well as deep psychological analysis, that our surface selves are only part of the deeper Self, and the latter is not entirely separate from the deeper Self of others. There is an element *in* us which transcends space and time, although it has to be expressed within it. But a fuller glimpse of this comes through those who take their prayer life seriously. Again and again they find they are "led" just at the right moment to someone whose need they can meet *precisely*. Again and again they find that in their own need help comes in the nick of time from unexpected sources, sometimes through a person, a sermon, a film at the cinema or a book that comes to their notice apparently "by chance". It is the *precise* relevance of such happenings which reveals an intelligent over-all pattern linking up apparently haphazard happenings.

If we are not looking for the connections, we may miss seeing them and also miss many opportunities of responding to this larger-scale "pattern" which can so enrich and fulfil our personal lives.

If, however, we once start looking for it, we do find evidence accumulates. The details may not always convince the hard-boiled, hard-headed man who will have "nothing to do with this nonsense". But the *results* are obvious to others. The proof here can only come to each one as he, or she, takes the *possibility* seriously enough to try to discern and respond to the Mind behind phenomena. We find evidence for this invisible pattern increases as we learn to trust its reality.

To use another analogy, iron filings fall into a precise pattern in the presence of a magnet near a higgledy-piggledy heap of them, which reveals the presence of an invisible "field of force" round the magnet. So if we seek to respond to the world of spirit we find the inter-relations with others form a network which is as real *in its own sphere* as the invisible field of force focused in a magnet. The analogy is apt, too, in that each filing which becomes magnetised is capable of attracting another filing. Each one who has tuned in spiritually extends the range of influence and makes it easier for others to respond too.

In all these ways we see there is a "pattern in the Cosmos" and the futility and triviality of so much of modern life—or mundane life in any age—falls away. We realise that *through* that very triviality great things are being wrought out. A great coral reef is the result of millions of colonies of polyps depositing their dead shells one upon another. An acorn grows into an oak: there are no oaks without acorns. So the cosmic Mind holds in its over-all pattern the majestic sweep of the stars, the long ages of pre-human evolution, the rise and fall of empires, the complexities of atoms, and the joys and sorrow of every human heart. So, throughout, the infinitely Great and the Infinitely Small are inter-related within the Reality which includes them both.

Further aspects of this Over-ruling Providence in the sphere of religious experience are considered in the next chapter.

# XI

# OVER-RULING PROVIDENCE AND RELIGIOUS EXPERIENCE

A SMALL CHILD ONE NIGHT REFUSED TO SAY HER PRAYERS. On being pressed as to the reason for this she said, "I don't like God. He's too big for me!" Many readers may have felt the same at some time or other. There is a tremendous sense of mystery and awe at times in religious experience. It seems to lift us for the moment right out of our ordinary sense of the precarious and changing elements of daily life into an atmosphere and a Presence so far beyond us that our finite, human lives seem to sink into complete insignificance before It. The psalmist felt it when saying, "What is man, that Thou art mindful of him?" Well has Professor Otto referred to God as *mysterium tremendum, mysterium fascinans.* Tremendous mystery, fascinating mystery.

Moses felt it as a command to "put off thy shoes from off thy feet for the place whereon thou standest is holy ground"[1] when a divine radiance enveloped the burning bush without consuming it. Isaiah felt it, saying, "Woe is me, for I am undone; because I am a man of unclean lips"[2] when he realised the presence of God. The three disciples felt it on the Mount of Transfiguration, when Christ was seen in such dazzling white robes, talking with Moses and Elijah.[3]

A light that can be seen, but which does not consume that which it envelops or irradiates, is often referred to in religious experience amongst people of all races and at various times. Always it seems to be the precursor to a call to some special

[1] Exodus 3, v. 5. [2] Isaiah 6, v. 5. [3] Luke 9, vv. 29–30.

service which is endorsed or sponsored by a higher power and not merely planned by the human agent on the purely natural level. Dr. Rebecca Beard, for example, described it as follows. "At first as I knelt by my bed and looked at the wall before me I saw a *black cross outlined there.* It was terribly black; there was no light in it. But as I groped and asked light came into that cross, and it was not light similar to the light of combustion. It was not a flame. I recall clearly that the outline of the cross was never blurred or indistinct as flames would have blurred it. Nothing leaped over the edge of it. *But it was white with a whiteness I cannot describe, for there is no whiteness that I know that is like it.* It was luminous and alive, but it was not fire nor flame as we see them".[1]

The whiteness that was alive, must have been similar to the dazzling whiteness on the Mount of Transfiguration.

I well remember an experience when such light broke through to me, flinging my arm in front of my eyes to shut out the blinding radiance. I can still in memory feel the roughness of a brushed woolly cardigan against my face, in the presence of a light that could not be shut out by a material arm covering my eyes. The fullness of the vision that followed marked a water-shed in my own life, as a new dimension of experience opened itself up to me.

It is, however, necessary not to expect all religious experience or illumination to take such visible, and almost tangible form. The reality of the presence and activity of God comes in many ways and many forms. Professor John Mackenzie, in the *British Weekly*, said he had received many letters from people who were puzzled, baffled and bewildered. People who wanted to—and did—pray, but *felt they were praying to someone who wasn't there.* They seemed to get no answer. Under the title used for this chapter I wrote an article as follows:[2]

[1] *Everyman's Mission*, p. 23. Publishers: Arthur James, Evesham.
[2] *British Weekly*, 1st Nov. 1956. Reproduced by permission of the Editor.

"I can fully sympathise with those who feel they are praying to 'Someone who isn't there'. Yet I think their failure to realise the all-pervading Presence of God may be due to thinking religious experience must be a *feeling* of a Presence transcending our own. That this can be felt at times, and by many people is true. Otto called it 'numinous', rising from a grisly demonic dread to the highest flights of mystical ecstasy as a strangely compelling experience, in which the experiencer cannot doubt he is in the presence of a Being greater than himself.

"True prayer does not necessarily involve this felt experience. Yet it does involve a measure of communion with the Creative Mind whose activities are manifest within this bewildering, baffling and wonderful world. Answers to our prayers do not always come while we are praying: but they may follow our prayers in such a way that we can see the connection later. For example, once when I was ill, I saw a second-hand filing cabinet for sale that would be very useful if I survived in a condition to use it: but I was not sure of doing so. Yet I did not want to lose the chance of it if I did survive. In prayer, I asked God if He approved of the 'buy' (which would also entail my recovery to make use of it) would He send me the five pounds to pay for it through *some channel I could not possibly foresee*.

"Within a week the five pounds arrived from a source that was completely unexpected! I have since made good use of the cabinet. I was not aware of God at the time of praying, but I had learned to look for answers to prayer that showed *they had registered in another mind than my own* in the outer and not only the inner world.

"This links together the over-ruling Providence of God and the nature of religious experience which Professor Mackenzie was referring to in answer to the many questioners in difficulties about both.

"Sometimes answers to prayer are not recognised because they flatly block some course of action on which we had set our heart. Yet later, we see that through that block, something far better became possible.

"In my book *Life, Faith and Prayer*[1] I wrote, 'There are many ways of treating such a subject as psychology and prayer. The method followed here is intended for those who believe in God and who all in varying ways pray to Him. The aim is to consider prayer in the light of the discoveries psychology has thrown on the ways our minds work in order that we may learn to pray more effectively. It is practical rather than theoretical, for the reader of average intelligence who desires to profit by the results of modern research and who is sure enough of God to realise all truth comes from Him.

" 'The part played by suggestion in meditation, by desire in petition, by imagination in bringing our wills into harmony with God, by faith in effective intercession, will be considered. Together with this, the psychological basis for penitence and the need for disciplined growth through moral effort is indicated. This leads on to the nature of worship and the goal of prayer, based on Our Lord's example as growing communion with "Our Father".

" 'The pre-supposition of communion is likeness of outlook, spiritual sympathy and moral unity of purpose. If prayer is to be a real communion with God, then it is only possible if God be self-revealing.'

"The many ways in which this self-revealing of a God who 'comes alive for us' are then described and might help the many who feel the emptiness of their prayers, and yet who continue to pray because the hunger of the human soul for communion with the God who made it is too real to be ignored.

"Professor Mackenzie also referred to Christ's prediction that He would rise again on the third day as an example of what psychical researchers would call pre-cognition. The recognition that various forms of extra-sensory perception, such as telepathy, clairvoyance, pre-cognition and telekinesis

[1] Allen and Unwin.

(the capacity to influence the movement of an external object without direct touch) may help us to bring the so-called 'miraculous' elements in biblical narratives into relation with our own modern knowledge. Instead of explaining them away we may see them at work to-day, although our idea of miracles has changed.

*Immensities*

"The more we learn of the complexity of the chemical reactions, for example, that go on in the growth of a rose which delights our eyes or nostrils, or the cabbage which is so mysteriously changed within us into our own physical tissues and capacity for thinking, the more we realise the 'Over-ruling Providence' which includes such precise detail on the infinitesimal scale with the vast immensities of the stellar universe. The light of the sun which is actively utilised by plants in their growth, on which our own nourishment depends, *eight minutes before was millions of miles away*.

"The intricacy of this inter-relatedness on the natural level may help us to realise the equal inter-relatedness on psychical and spiritual levels involved in human nature. The effects of prayer not only in our own lives, but through intercession in the lives of others, become more intelligible in light of this.

"There seems to be a growing network of reciprocal influence amongst those whose prayer life is *disciplined and persistent* which enables God to bring about results that transcend contingencies on the natural level by bringing them within the scope of a more far-reaching 'pattern' of Grace. Evidence for this is increasing from many sources.

"This would seem to be the sphere within which the overruling Providence of God shapes our lives, from within and from without, so that we may find our ultimate fulfilment in contributing the tiny fragment possible to us where and as we are, within the fellowship of the whole humanity of which we are each a part.

"Each of us is a focus for growth and development on the natural level, with a part to play in the historical continuity of all mankind. But each of us is also a focus through which the Eternal significance of the temporal and contingent is distilled and taken up into God, through the Christ who so lived on earth that He took the fullness of His manhood into God as only God could do."

### *A Practical Illustration*

Perhaps an example of an "Over-ruling Providence" may help to make this clearer.

Some time ago a friend wished to sell a small business run by herself and her husband. They advertised it without any one taking any notice. She then wrote to ask my prayers on their behalf. They felt sure it was right to retire from this and had seen the place for their next venture. On taking their need up into the Presence of God, my mind was held very deeply for about half an hour in the silence that transcends discursive thought, but yet which involves a more intense concentration than our everyday activities demand. After it I felt some process of inter-communication had been initiated that would eventually lead to the right person for that particular business being led to buy it.

I wrote to my friend to that effect, and that I was sure there was a *specific* person for whom it would be as right for him to take it as for them to leave it.

Shortly afterwards the first applicant for the business turned up and made a firm offer. They decided to accept it, though not liking the man or feeling he was the right kind to build on the foundations they had laid. Later, he withdrew his offer and they felt a sense of relief, in spite of being left without a purchaser. Then another applicant came, who seemed eminently suitable and they were overjoyed, feeling this must be the answer to prayers. But this one eventually did not buy.

A third party then turned up, decided to buy and, though they felt as with the first applicant that he was not really the right kind of person, they agreed to sell.

Then came a big blow. The buyer withdrew his offer and they were left high and dry, with furniture already packed to go into temporary rooms, as the house they wanted would not be available for another three months.

My friend wrote in great perplexity and distress. Again I was held in the silence as I took the need into my own heart sufficiently to raise it to God. Again there was the assurance that there was a particular person for that business, and also a realisation that my friends had made two mistakes that were preventing the final links in the network to bring the buyer and the business together. The first was in accepting an offer from someone unsuitable for the kind of good will they had built up, instead of waiting until someone right for it came along. The second was in not realising that as the next home for them would not be available for another three months, God might want them to carry on rather than being at a loose end in unsuitable rooms. I wrote to say this and that if they could continue to trust God, the right buyer *would* come in time and in the meantime they were needed where they were.

My friend then wrote to say she *was* trusting, and was sure God had prevented the wrong people for the work buying the business. All the distress and tension had gone out of her letter so I realised God could now meet the real need with some real lessons learned. Within a few days this was confirmed. A previous employee who had for some time wished for this particular business, "accidentally" heard it was for sale and dashed round at once to try to secure it.

With this the whole "pattern" fell into line. They *knew* he would build on their foundations and he could wait the three months until they could rightly move into their next venture. This confirmed my intuition that there was a *specific* individual for whom that niche was prepared, without knowing who it would be.

This is quoted in considerable detail, as it shows so very clearly the influence of an over-ruling intelligence at work, until the ways that would not fulfil its aims were blocked and the one that could was brought into being to the *real* satisfaction of all these parties—my friends, the buyer, and the seller of the place they wished to buy instead.

If we can work with God that is the kind of solution to expect, not one that is at the expense of anyone else, but which fulfils the real needs of *all* those concerned.

It may help many who find unexpected barriers in the way of something they are sure it is right to do, to realise these may be essential to bring about the *one* way that meets the needs of others as well as their own. It is a real, and recent, example that "All things work together for good to those who love God and are called according to His purpose." This is considered further in the next chapter.

## XII

# THE CHAIN-MAIL OF THE SPIRIT

THE IDEA OF THE "CHAIN-MAIL OF THE SPIRIT" WOVEN LINK by link, flashed into my mind the other day during meditation. It brought with it a realisation of the reality of the life and experience which enabled St. Paul to refer to the "breast-plate of righteousness" and the "shield of faith". The true life of the spirit expresses the same ideas in terms relevant to the experience of each. When taking shape thus within us we know we are in touch with the living reality through which earlier symbols were coined in a way that repeating the original words does not give. Such new symbols arising spontaneously within us bring with them the realisation that they are the equivalents of similar insights into spiritual realities which had issued in words that had lived for centuries. They bring with them the sense of kinship, of fellowship, of shared participation in the spiritual life of all who had made that level of realisation their own.

We have to assimilate and make the experience our own before it can flash through in *fresh* terms in us. The "chain-mail of the Spirit" is a creative idea, with innumerable ramifications and possibilities.

Chain-mail is woven link by link: each interlaced with its immediate neighbours. The fineness of its links makes for great flexibility: yet its strength is considerable. Its purpose is defensive, not aggressive. It is worn to protect all the vulnerable parts of the body without, like massive defensive armour, impeding activity. Like the shield of faith, it protects from external evil.

The chain-mail of the spirit must be woven through the inter-action of those living by the spirit, woven in life, by love with patience. Every real relationship, hammered out and held through whatever difficulties it involves, forms a link in this chain-mail of the spirit.

There is a solidarity of mankind on the natural level. Even conflicts between man and man, man and woman, nation and nation, imply a common level of humanity. There is no conflict in that sense between a man and the insect which bites him and on which he treads. These imply differing orders of life, each following their own nature without reference to moral principles. Man does not feel it incumbent on him to nurture and nourish insect life, except when, as in the case of bees, he wants the honey they produce. Animals dangerous to human life he kills: those whose strength, skill, flesh or milk he can use, he domesticates.

But conflicts between men and nations are civil war within mankind. The man who kills another kills something in himself. The man who degrades another, degrades himself. We all share in a common inheritance, linked through our parents with all their ancestors. We are also linked through the social traditions with the life of tribe, race or nation. To be human is to be born into a family, by the joint action of man and woman, whether the man repudiates his responsibility, throwing the burden in double measure on the woman, or whether he shares it as a privilege. To be human is to be born into some particular culture, whether primitive or civilised, stable or in rapid transition, whether maturing or disintegrating.

To be human is to be born in one place at one specific time, of one particular colour, whether white, red, yellow, black or any of the inter-minglings that occur.

To be human is thus to be at the same time a *distinctive* individual, and yet to participate in a *common nature*.

True sanity (and sanctity) involves the recognition of the equal importance of *both* factors.

To become great is only to realise the maximum possibilities within humanity, not to be superior to them. Dictators and demi-gods *betray* their humanity and in the end are destroyed by their failure to be true to the "human pact". Loyalty to those who have lived before and our duties towards those who will come after us, and inherit both the good and evil we leave behind are essential for sanity.

But there is also another kind of solidarity in human life. This is not something given willy-nilly, independently of the way in which we live our lives. It arises through awareness of what seems to be another dimension of being. Misused though the word is, spirit is still probably the best term we can use to refer to this. It has been recognised in all ages and in the most primitive cultures, though descriptions and apprehensions vary, since they can only take shape within the level of knowledge and experience, as well as the mental capacity of those concerned.

Spirit seems to transcend the particularity of the individual human being, linking him in some way with a Greater Spirit responsible both for his human existence and for that of the world in which he lives. It also transcends the particular social environment within which each human being is born as a member. It also seems to transcend the natural level of humanity itself, apart from awareness of its potential participation within the life of the Spirit.

Yet awareness of it only arises through living within our human limitations, and realising our potentialities as fully as possible.

Not all individuals awaken to the reality of this all pervasive Presence, encompassing our lesser minds. But from all times of which we have any record, whether verbal or inferred from tombs and holy places, *some* have sensed and responded to this world of Spirit and found life fuller because of it.

The fellowship of the spirit, the recognition of similar experiences in all ages, races and climes, brings a sense of unity amongst mankind, in distinction from the particularity, temporality and partiality of individual human beings. Apprehensions of this wider world within which mankind itself falls can only be expressed symbolically in human language. Symbols thrown up in genuine religious experience, however, tend to awaken recognition of their source beyond that of the individual mind in others. This opens the way for those others to share in such experience themselves.

Human history is not only a record of attempts to survive physically against the forces of storm, flood, pestilence or famine. It includes the record of spiritual explorations in this other dimension of being which gives significance to man's efforts not just to live like an animal, contained in nature. Man seeks to live better, to seek a fuller life, to create, to conserve, and to enjoy sharing thoughts, hopes, aspirations and achievements with his peers, i.e. with those capable of appreciation of the level of life concerned through participating in it.

It is as if the natural framework is given within the world of nature including mankind, with the possibility of responding to inspiration from the Creative Mind responsible for both, in such a way as to bring harmony out of the conflicts and confusions on the natural level.

It has often been said that though men and women seem separate individuals, they may be like peaks in a mountain range, joined together at their base. It is not perhaps so often realised that as peaks differ in size from small foothills to the heights of Everest, those highest up may catch more of the inspiration of the spirit than those on the plains or amidst the foothills of the "mass mind". They may then reflect something of the eternal down into the plains to guide the less mature. We are joined together from above as well as from below.

The "chain-mail of the spirit" is woven link by link by those awakened to the reality of the Spirit.

There would thus be a solidarity of mankind on the natural

level and a solidarity of mankind *to be achieved* on the spiritual level in proportion to the response to the Guiding Spirit who sees and plans the whole and the particular function of every part within it. Those reaching even a glimmer of this plan would in fact find themselves more closely attuned to others who had also glimpsed it than to those in the natural groupings of family or clan.

There is a ground plan of the structure of the universe laid down within it which is being progressively discovered by scientists. Such discovery has enabled man to make much fuller use of natural resources: though with the increased range of destructive ones this is a two-edged weapon.

To use increased resources for the welfare of mankind and not in civil war within it, needs the recognition of the dimension of the spirit that fulfils humanity by relating it to its true source in the Mind of God. This makes of every man a potential brother whom to hurt or kill is as to hurt or kill oneself. But the potentiality has to be actualised not in mass feeling for the many who are unknown, but by real links with those with whom we come into touch.

The discoveries of science can be rendered available through impersonal channels. The life of the spirit can only be fostered by those in whom it is a reality. Life can only be fulfilled on earth as each contributes its quota to the welfare of mankind as a trust from the God from whom the gifts of science and natural resources, as well as the gifts of the Spirit in and through persons, both come.

## XIII

# THE GOOD THAT HAS NO OPPOSITE

THIS MORNING THERE CAME A DEEP REALISATION THAT "THE Good that has no opposite" really *is* good and *can only create good*: that it is impossible for it to create evil. The evils on the level on which good and evil seem to be in conflict and to be irreconcilable were seen to fall within the range of "Good which has no opposite" in such a way that, by the overcoming of the relative evils that do actually arise in our present experience, a greater good is achieved than if they had not been allowed in the picture at all. They were not *created* as such by God: they were, in Hughling Jackson's phrase, "release phenomena" when the control of higher centres of being was lacking.[1]

Such symptoms of disorder are not of the true nature of being and so the Reality of Being is always in ultimate control of the whole realm. Its potentialities, perversions and distortions are so interrelated that the very "release phenomena" of disorder lead to the search for the higher "order of being"

[1] Jackson was a physiologist who discovered that when the higher brain centres were out of action the functions of the lower brain centres, which had previously been controlled by them in the service of health and wholeness, broke down into symptoms of disorder which he called "release phenomena". These could be studied and even treated as symptoms, but could only disappear completely *if the higher control re-asserted itself*. The highest control comes through the development of the spirit, and this is shown in some cases of the spiritual healing of organic diseases, which were "release phenomena," not normal functions. Hooker gives a similar analogy. "To disobey your proper law [i.e. the law God makes for a being such as you] means to find yourself obeying one of God's lower laws: e.g. if when walking on a slippery pavement you neglect the law of Prudence, you suddenly find yourself obeying the laws of gravitation." Quoted as from Hooker, by C. S. Lewis, *The Problem of Pain*, p. 70

that could heal, regenerate or transmute them. The Good that is beyond or above the opposites that are in conflict is also *within* them as the urge to their own transcendence, not by exclusion, but by inclusion. The very conflict which so often seems insoluble and intolerable, since we cannot eliminate either side, nor see how to reconcile them, is due to the reality of one form of the Good which is essential for the whole in *each* of the conflicting elements. That is why we feel so torn between the apparent opposites until we cease to pit them against each other as if either could obliterate or overcome the other. Then, when we seek the "good above the opposites", gathering all our resources together in the search for "wholeness", we find the nature of these opposites changes from the "release phenomena" due to either expressed in isolation or antagonism, to their *true* nature when polarised in harmony. The form of this cannot be foreseen from the stage of conflict. Something genuinely *new* comes into being when a true resolution of mental or emotional conflict is found on a higher plane of Being.

The idea of this is not new, of course, and many times the "Good that has no opposite", the Good beyond our relative earthly conflicts of good and evil, has been sought. But this morning it came with a deeper significance as *always* operative. It was a Good that could only create a Good, could only bring good out of and through *all* its creations in the long run. No created being was evil in itself. Only when out of relation with the wider whole could it bring symptoms of disorder into being *within the range of its potential activity.* The range of each was seen to be limited by the ultimate nature of the Good so that it inevitably produced reactions *within a wider environment* through which in time the disorder could be rightly related to the potentialities it was distorting.

Yet this is no mechanical or automatic process. It is a vital interaction, involving suffering as well as joy; distress as well as delight. Yet in a very real sense it is a process in which the creative element, the good that can only create good, sees through the temporary disorder, the sin, the suffering, to the good that can be elicited within it. A doctor, for example, may say something is distressing to watch. Yet while even inflicting pain his primary consciousness is on the beneficial, not the painful, side of it, so that he can keep calm and detached enough to "bind up the broken hearted" as well as the broken limbed.

There is thus, as Jesus stressed, a fundamental joy in creation that not all the consequences of the "sins, negligences and ignorances" of man can finally mar. We have made too much of the suffering of Christ on the Cross, not because it was not real enough (it may even have been far greater than our narrow minds can conceive) but because it was a *remedial activity within the wider framework of the Creativity of the Father-Godhead which was primary*. Christ, for the Joy that was set before Him, endured the Cross. It was that *voluntary* element in it which was greater than all the massed forces of disorder and of the vested interests in maintaining that disorder as the only level of life then known. This brought to earth, really incarnate, a new principle of life which was capable of harmonising even the destructive and disintegrating forces of death. The very stuff of Christ's Body was transmuted into the "Body of His Resurrection". This was akin to, yet transcending, the limitations of the old.

The early Church was alive and dynamic because the emphasis was on the Resurrection, on the Good News, on the Power of the Holy Spirit. The veil separating the Holy of Holies from the worshippers in the Temple had been rent from top to bottom. The way to God—to the "Good that has no opposite"—was open. Yet later the emphasis fell too much on the heinousness of sin and the need to placate an angry Jehovah by Christ's sacrifice. Whereas the true emphasis should be on the fact that God so loved that He gave the Christ, to win us to Himself; and, as St. Paul said, with Him gave all else needful for our salvation, our wholeness. The compassion of Christ expresses the compassion of the Father. "I and the Father are One", He said. Within that all-inclusive love we all come. Young and old, rich and poor, sinner or saint, male or female, sick or well: Moslem, Hindu, Buddhist or Christian. That love will not let us go till it *has* blessed us and brought us to the fulfilment of the potentialities of our being within the fellowship of the communion of saints. This is an interaction infinitely transcending the limited range shown by the "release phenomena" of our average egocentric life. It transforms the latter into a richness and complexity of harmonious integration within the Whole that awes us into humility while lifting us up into a harmony with the "Good which has no opposite". This is pledged by its very nature to redeem and sanctify those whom it has created capable of recognising and responding to the call to the self-transcendence of love, which is the only true self-fulfilment.

We must now try to see some of the ways in which God carries out His creative work, redeeming and sanctifying (making whole, holy, spiritually mature) our human lives.

## XIV

# IN HIS NAME

"WHATSOEVER YE SHALL ASK THE FATHER IN MY NAME, HE will give it to you." That is apparently a blank cheque on a Heavenly Father. What did Christ mean by "in His name"? We often add "through Jesus Christ our Lord" or "in Christ's Name" to our prayers, and yet the answer of so amazing a promise, that *whatsoever* we ask in His name will be given, does not follow.

The phrase "in His name" is central to this. The idea of this chapter came into my mind as a result of being asked to write a foreword to a book. Could I honestly put my name to it or not? Putting my name to a book involved a responsibility. Sometimes I could recommend someone's work, sometimes I could not honestly do so.

Giving one's name entails real responsibilities on many levels. A commonplace one is putting our signature on a cheque when there is a sufficient balance in our account to cover the amount so that the bank can rightly "honour our cheques".

Obviously, therefore, "in Christ's Name" will only include those things He really can endorse and can put His name to *without reserve*. It cannot apply to mixed requests, the answers to which would produce results He did not want or which would clash with the real needs of others. It isn't enough to add "in Christ's name" to *any* request and expect magical results. Yet Christ obviously meant us to take Him at His Word and to expect God to honour cheques "in His Name".

Three possible levels of interpretation may help us to learn how to pray with power.

First we have the life and example of Christ as a guide to the kind of things to which He could put his name. This would rule out the prayer quoted by Professor Glenn Clark as the wrong kind. A man came to him and said hc was "through with prayer" because he had prayed for a victory over a rival and the rival had won. Dr. Clark asked if he had *needed* the victory more than his rival. He said no, but he *wanted* to discomfort his rival. We can't expect God to honour prayers with that motive in them.

But we can expect Him to bless and use *all* prayers inspired by real love of another. When Jesus was "moved with compassion", things began to happen and many sick folk were healed. If prayers with real love in them are not answered in the form we want or expect, we can be sure God will use that love to meet a deeper need than the one we could see. We are members of a family, interacting at many points, and some answers to prayer cannot come completely until some human co-operation is forthcoming, whether by faith, skill or love. Nor can answers to prayer come at the expense of others. "In His Name" brings to mind the Lord's own prayer, "Our Father". Selfish, self-centred prayers cannot get past or round that family clause.

Secondly, we have the lessons of history, the way in which the leaven of Christianity is slowly permeating humanity so that we can say some things are "unchristian", even though as yet our capacity to respond "christianly" is inadequate to prevent them. We also see that some things once thought to be Christian, e.g. the Inquisition, were in fact unchristian. They were distortions of Christianity, things not in Christ's name at all. On a long view we can see things in a clearer perspective and increasingly separate the wheat and the tares which had grown up together. So we may see more clearly what we may "ask in His name".

Thirdly, the *Name* in Christ's day was significant of the real inner being, the reality itself, and not just a symbol. The

Hebrew scriptures are full of the importance of names. This was shown in their story of the Garden of Eden. When they said Adam named the animals this meant to them that he saw into their nature and so could name them and control that which he could name. At critical points in their history a new name was given. Abraham's wife Sarai became Sarah when she was about to bear a son, Isaac, in her old age. Jacob became Israel after his all-night wrestle with an angel who then said, "Thy name shall be called no more Jacob but Israel: for thou hast striven with God and with men and hast prevailed."[1]

The early Hebrews never spoke the name of God. It was too sacred an intrusion on the Divine Reality. They were also forbidden to make any images of God, which could only distort or misrepresent Him. "I am that I am" was God's cognomen, and Moses was told to say "I am" hath spoken.

Then came Jesus of Nazareth, a village carpenter, who won[2] the title of Christ, the Messiah, in a religious world in which names meant so much more than they have degenerated into to-day. When He asked Peter "Whom say ye that I am?" his reply "the Christ, the Son of the living God" meant more than even yet we have fully realised. "I am that I am" became "Christ", a name we *could* use. The awe-inspiring God, whom no created image could hold, took a form that could be truly named. The Son of the living God expressed the essence and Reality of Divinity within an actual historical Incarnation and united the seen and the unseen, the temporal and the eternal, in a way no lesser name or image could do.

Here at last we see the secret of His Promise, "Whatsoever

[1] Genesis, 32. v. 28.

[2] This is not meant to imply that this was only a human achievement. But God had to bring the insight into the reality of the Messiah (from above or beyond) within the framework of the thought of the day in the nation prepared for His coming. So Christ had to win the title on earth or fail to make the break-in from the Divine a reality to or for us. We need at every point to see both the human and the divine aspects of that One life, if the reality of it is to express the newness of life in Christ when we respond to Him as Redeemer of, and from, the old unregenerate life.

ye shall ask the Father *in my name*, He will give it you." The name was the consciousness, the being the I-amness of one who *knew* there was the power to perform all that could reach that central focus of God on earth. In Him the Divine image in man was one with its Divine source, undistorted and undeflected by sins, negligences or ignorances.

In Christ, in His Name, His essential being, all desires incompatible with the true nature of both God and man, and of all other created forms of life or being, were eliminated.

The temptations in the wilderness showed the respect of God for His own laws. Not even to satisfy the hunger of Christ must stones be turned into bread. Not even to make a spectacular impact on the imagination of the people could He throw Himself from the temple and expect to be miraculously saved from the consequences of falling. Not even to rule the world He came to save must He take the prestige of the kingdoms of this world on Satan's terms, without the real power that can only come from *within the true being* of God or man.

So, as we learn of Him, as our self-centred desires are gradually sifted out from our deeper spiritual needs, we may begin to pray "in His name" and find our real needs *are* met in ways we could never have foreseen. We may ask for much less than we used to do: but that *less*, which is our real need, *is* met. Reality does honour cheques truly drawn "in Christ's Name".

So, as the name means so much, Saul of Tarsus became Paul after his conversion on the road to Damascus. The new man in Christ needed a new name to symbolise the death of the old self and the birth of the new Christian one.

To allow one's friends to use one's Christian name was at one time a great privilege. It involved a sense of intimacy with the real inner person, a real friendship not shared with mere acquaintances, with whom one was sociable but not intimate. The habit of "hail fellow well met", with Christian names flung about at first meetings without time to know whether a real community of interest and mutual respect is possible, cheapens personality. In a real sense, by its *familiarity without real acquaintance*, it depersonalises those who drop into it automatically. Yet where the Name of Christ is a living reality, the sharing of a Christian name in its real sense with friends deepens the friendship and quickens the inner reality through which each is participating, in however small a measure, in fellowship with and service of Christ Himself.

Christ said, "Where two or three are gathered together 'In my name' there am I in the midst of them." When one hundred and twenty people were gathered together "with one accord" in His name, the Divine outpouring of the Holy Spirit at Pentecost swept away all barriers. Disciples who had previously fled and left their Master in His hour of betrayal and need, became empowered in His name to risk their own lives in His service until all men should see the glory of God in the face of Christ Jesus.

## XV

# THE INVISIBLE CHRIST

THOSE OF YOU WHO SAW THE FILM OF H. G. WELLS' *The Invisible Man* may have been impressed, as I was, by the scene in which fresh footsteps in the snow appeared *one by one* exactly as if someone *was* walking over it, yet without any other sign of the presence of the invisible man who was actually making them on otherwise untrodden snow.

Though there was nothing to show *how* they appeared before our eyes, it was obvious from the fact that imprints were left in the snow that something that was invisible was *real* in some sense. Imaginary figures may disport themselves in dreams and phantasies, but they don't leave footprints behind that can even be photographed.

So it is with Christ. From the time He ceased to be visible to His disciples, saying it was expedient for them that He should go away in order that the Holy Spirit should come and lead them into all Truth, we keep coming across *His* footprints. These often come in unexpected ways or places, showing the reality of the "Invisible Christ" breaking through into the actualities of our world of space and time, making fresh tracks that we can follow, step by step, as they come into sight.

Those who have learned to recognise His influence through the many and varied channels He uses find life fuller and richer. Yet they also find life full of surprises. Just when they seem to be sure some particular channel really is conveying His touch, in forgiveness, in healing, in opening the way through some special tangle, or meeting some special need, He seems to withdraw from it. The invisible Presence seems to have departed and life drops down to everyday levels again. We cannot doubt He had been transfiguring this, but the old prayers, the old attitudes, do not seem to work any longer. The life seems to have gone out of them.

It is very rarely that we realise what this means and that it is not necessarily something wrong with us or with our circumstances, but that it is a real confirmation that something—or Someone—had been active behind the scenes before. We need to be able to recognise Him in less familiar ways. To begin to rely on what can be seen and expected almost as a matter of course is to lose the *invisible source* of all that was of value in the happenings.

This is just the lesson His disciples had to learn after the Ascension, in order that they might become responsive to a wider and fuller inspiration through the Holy Spirit, the Spirit of Christ Himself.

So if the light seems to be withdrawn, and prayers no longer "come alive" and glow with a meaning greater than can actually be expressed, let us take it that the Invisible Christ is trying to make us realise Him in another way. If instead of trying to go back to the old we are willing to go forward, we suddenly discover *His* footprints in that very attempt to be faithful in the absence of the sense of His presence that had made the earlier period after conversion such a joy. To rejoice when aware of Christ is good, but to be faithful when that awareness is withdrawn until we can recognise Him in another guise is better. Always the invisible Christ is there; always He is leaving His footprints to link the visible and the invisible. But just as the invisible man was more than the footprints in the snow, so Christ is more than *any* of the signs through which we recognise Him. When He ceases to use a sign we have begun to rely on, it is only to lead us to recognise Him through another so that we do not mistake the footprint we can see for the Mighty One Who made it.

The great mystics have all realised this. The first rapture

as the reality of Spirit, of a life transcending space and time, was realised transformed the whole world in which they lived. This was followed by a deeper, more awesome beauty in the "Dark Night of the Soul". During this period, the process occurs of shifting the centre of gravity, the central focus of personal life, from the egoistic, or even the social, to the spiritual level which underlies and upholds all forms and lower levels of personal or social life. This goes deeper than even the best in our own particular culture, whatever that may be, which is why there is a common kinship between the genuine mystics of different ages and races which shows they have shared some developmental experience in common.

The stresses of ordinary adolescence are nothing in comparison with these deeper shifts of interest and consecration, through which the whole level of life is eventually raised for those who persist and persevere in their efforts. This is then followed by the serenity and assurance and maturity of the later life, which ushers in a creative period that may go on right into old age.

This is a creativity of spirit. It is a creativity expressed in fellowship, a fellowship which is concerned primarily with the quality of human life and relationships. In it love supersedes force, and the prestige of "position" no longer buttresses up a weak ego. The inner reality, wrought out in the heat of the conflict, is the sole measure of the range of its influence and the quality of the life of the Spirit which is radiated through it. It would seem that Christ Himself passed through such an experience during the temptations in the wilderness before the Carpenter of Nazareth began His mission to the whole world, seen and unseen alike.

In the first phase of awareness of the truth and reality of Christ the outward results are obvious and many. It is as if God gives them as outward proofs of the Reality we have just glimpsed. Moreover, others find help and healing through us. Then comes a change. It is a call to a different and higher form of service. At first we are bewildered and struggle with greater and greater effort with less and less result, and think the wrong in us must be blocking the way for God. But in time these blinkers are withdrawn and we shy about startled and confused, and long for the old days of apparently effortless insight and power. But we are growing up—or perhaps being grown up might better express the shaping by a greater and wiser mind than our own—through this turmoil. If this is accepted and faced as a stage of growth and not thought of as a moral failure, this period has a wild and terrible beauty of its own as a new and deeper pattern is being etched within us until we become able to see for ourselves. *Inner sight then becomes really our own, not just a deposit transmitted by others.*

This is followed by a third phase. The function of this is not that of going out to deal with those who have fallen by the wayside, but is on the preventive level, forestalling much that would otherwise issue in disease, disorder or disaster. This is never spectacular as some healings or conversions are. Yet those who participate in such interior activity are aware that much of the invisible activity of Christ is done through those who have stood their ground and their test. They then no longer need to see the outward signs to convince them of His presence when His invisible footsteps are being made.

The influence of those who have reached this third phase of maturity is again unconscious and effortless, as in the first period. But it is manifested behind the scenes, so to speak. There is an anonymity, an unselfconsciousness about it, which is more effective than self-assertion. Influence is then less direct, the fruits are not so apparent to the eyes of the world. But the "good seed" is sown more widely and takes root whenever the ground of some human soul is ready to let just that particular seed germinate. Moreover, instead of seeking out those who need help, those whose need they really can meet are guided to come to them at just the right time. Ways do open out again after the "Dark Night of the Soul" has been lived through in a veritable life-and-death struggle with themselves. They have learned to see through all outward signs—all the footprints of Christ—to the Invisible Reality of Christ Himself.

How many such cycles may occur, as some fresh beauty and challenge of the Spirit calls us to embody it, we who are only among the foothills of the Spirit cannot foresee. But to have glimpsed and experienced the deep rhythms of life involved on any such level, enables us to press steadily upwards and forwards until the Divine Pattern is fully revealed and every fragment falls into its right place within the Beauty of the Whole, the Kingdom of God in its fullness.

To discover such a pattern being woven amidst the cross-currents of life, to realise the necessity for periods of expansion and periods of consolidation prior to another advance, is to share in the rhythms of Life itself and so find the footprints of the Invisible Christ everywhere.

# L'ENVOIE

SO THE MYSTERY OF AND VICTORY OVER SUFFERING IS A WAY OF life. As the grand old man of Lambaréné, Dr. Albert Schweitzer, says, in *The Quest of the Historical Jesus*.

"He comes to us as one unknown, without a name, as of old by the Lakeside. He came to those men who knew Him not. He speaks to us the same word 'Follow thou me!' and sets us to the tasks which He has to fulfil for our time. He commands. And to those who obey Him, whether they be wise or simple, He will reveal Himself in the toils, the conflicts, the sufferings which they shall pass through in His fellowship, and, as in an ineffable mystery, they shall learn in their own experience who He is."

CHRIST THE HOPE OF THE WORLD
IN TIME AND IN ETERNITY.